HIDDEN
BEDROOM
PARTNERS

HIDDEN BEDROOM PARTNERS

Needs and Motives that Destroy Sexual Pleasure

Frank Hajcak, Ph.D.
and
Patricia Garwood, M.S.

Libra Publishers, Inc.

First Edition

Library of Congress Catalog No. 84-62865

Copyright © 1987 by Frank Hajcak and Patricia Garwood

Manufactured in the United States of America

ISBN 0-87212-190-9

Libra Publishers, Inc.
3089C Clairemont Dr., Suite 383, San Diego, California 92117

Contents

PART I NONSEXUAL SEX

Preface   vii
1. What Is Nonsexual Sex?   3
2. Using Sex to Get Affection   10
3. Avoiding Intimacy Through Sex   15
4. Avoiding Loneliness Through Sex   24
5. Sex for Atonement   31
6. Sex to Safeguard Fidelity   38
7. Sex to Confirm Sexuality   46
8. Sex and Self-esteem   55
9. Sex and Guilt   65
10. Sex to Mask Anger   74
11. Sex for Revenge   81
12. Jealousy and Sex   87
13. Sex Motivated by Boredom   98
14. Sex for Dominance and Control   105
15. Sex as a Haven   115
16. Sex and Social Pressure   119
17. Sex as a Buffer for Depression   125
18. Sex as Rebellion   132

PART II UNDERSTANDING NONSEXUAL SEX

19. How It Happens   145
20. Why It Continues   152
21. The Dangers of Nonsexual Sex   161

PART III DISCOVERING SEXUAL SEX

22. Sexual Sex: What Is It Like?   175
23. Exploring Your Sex Life   181
24. Understanding Sexuality   191
25. Putting Sex in Its Proper Perspective   196
26. Putting It All Together   206

Appendix I. Nonsexual Sex Therapy:
General Guidelines   209
Appendix II. Nonsexual Sex Therapy:
Goals and Considerations   219
Bibliography   225
Index   227

Preface

Why do couples lose interest in one another sexually? Why does sexual enthusiasm decline with age? Why do so many seemingly good marriages fall apart in later years? Why do couples often feel that something is missing from their sex lives? Why doesn't everybody enjoy sex as much as they think they should?

We believe the answer to all these is that the bedroom is being used as a battleground. Freud taught us that much of human behavior is motivated by repressed sexual needs. We start with the premise that a great deal of our sexual behavior is motivated by repressed or hidden nonsexual needs. We have sex when we really want and need something else, such as affection, intimacy, companionship, a haven from stress or boredom, or a release from pent-up anger. The satisfaction and pleasure derived from the sex act must be divided among these hidden needs. Thus, none are completely satisfied as they all fight for their share.

There are two consequences: First, sex loses much of its natural pleasure. Eventually couples think they have a sex problem when, in fact, they do not. Second, by focusing on the sexual, they can never resolve the underlying emotional conflict. They are doomed to re-enact the same battle. Eventually they throw in the towel on a relationship that could have been saved.

This deterioration of the sexual relationship not only can be stopped; it can be reversed. By weeding nonsexual needs out of the bedroom, we can restore and increase sexual pleasure and satisfaction a hundredfold. That's what this book is about. It is a guide for discovering sexual sex—sex that is not burdened by emotional needs.

We have included enough theory and process so that it also can serve as a comprehensive guide for therapists, counselors, and educators, and be useful in courses on human sexuality. It is also a handbook for parents who wish to enlighten their teenagers about the nonsexual reasons for sexual activities.

During adolescence the foundations of our sex lives are formed. Abuses and bad habits learned during these formative years will be carried into adulthood. If teenagers remain ignorant of how sex is misused, we condemn them to years of neurotic, nonsexual sex.

The book is divided into three parts. Part I explains how nonsexual emotional needs inhibit sexual pleasure and satisfaction. Seventeen nonsexual motives are discussed, and at the end of each chapter suggestions are offered on the prevention or alleviation of the problems created by each motive.

Part II explains how we learn to misuse sex in order to satisfy nonsexual needs, and discusses the danger of continuing to do so.

Part III is a guide for achieving sexual sex. Included are:

—Questionnaires to aid in the systematic examination of one's sex life and discover the hidden motives which lurk at the bedroom door.
—A table to delineate the difference between love and sex.
—A discussion on the myths of the bedroom personality.
—A discussion on the difference between pleasure and satisfaction and blocking and holding back.
—A list of the many benefits that can be reaped by keeping nonsexual needs out of the bedroom.

HIDDEN BEDROOM PARTNERS

PART I

NONSEXUAL SEX

1

What Is Nonsexual Sex?

Did you ever feel let down or disappointed after sex? Most of us have, and not known why. We may have blamed the situation, mood, partner, or questioned our sexual adequacy. In fact, dissatisfaction with sex often results from something very different: HAVING SEX FOR NONSEXUAL REASONS! You have sex when you really want or need something else. Let us explain.

Sex is designed by nature to afford intense mental and physical pleasure. In the natural order of things, when sexual needs arise, we respond directly and appropriately. In this simplistic context, sex delivers the pleasure for which it was designed.

Through the process of socialization we have created social, moral, and personal inhibitions which restrict the natural flow of sexual behavior. Sex has become entangled with needs and desires which have little or nothing to do with it; for example, our need for affection and love, for reassurance and security, to feel masculine or feminine, to feel special or to avoid loneliness. When sex is used to satisfy any of these needs, much of the pleasure it can afford is lost. Sex simply cannot satisfy nonsexual needs. Consequently, these needs remain unfulfilled and we feel frustrated after sex.

Since we are aware of our sexual desires and unaware of these other needs, we blame sex for our dissatisfaction. In fact, sex has little to do with this frustration. Sex was abused. We have used it as a vehicle for the expression of nonsexual needs.

Let us explore the issue further by asking what may seem an absurd question: Have you ever tried to satisfy your hunger or thirst by having sex? You're probably thinking, "Of course not! It would be crazy to try." Undoubtedly you would end up feeling unsatisfied, frustrated, and probably hungrier. Sex surely would have lost some of the enjoyment it affords. In this case, since you were aware of the hunger, you probably would not blame sex for the lack of fulfillment.

However, most nonsexual needs that we try to satisfy in the bedroom are more subtle. We are not aware of them. We are aware only of a desire for sex. Thus, after sex, we attribute the dissatisfaction or frustration to poor sex.

These nonsexual motives are like partners with whom you must share the pleasures of sex. The stronger the nonsexual need and the less you are aware of its presence, the bigger the share of pleasure it will grab. In a sense you are in competition with these motives. The prize is sexual pleasure and satisfaction. The more they get, the less you get, and the less satisfying your sex life becomes. Eventually sex will be reduced to a chore which yields little pleasure.

Consider the following examples:

Marion, a musician, moved to New York City to further her career. She was lonely and missed her family and friends. A few weeks later, after dinner, she invited her male companion home for a drink, rather than face another evening alone. They had sex and the mechanics went well. Yet, Marion felt unsatisfied and surprised at her low level of enjoyment. She blamed it on her lack of sexual prowess. She began to question her capacity to enjoy sex.

In fact, her lack of enjoyment had little to do with her sexual skill or capacity for pleasure. The decrease in enjoyment was due to the interference of the nonsexual need for companionship. She was sharing her bedroom pleasure with this hidden partner.

Paul was a 32-year-old, recently divorced executive. His wife had left him for another man, seven years his senior. He was stunned. In their angry exchanges she called him a lousy lover. Because he was a "free and horny man" (so he thought), he began a series of seductions. After a few months of this activity, he realized that sex was not as good as he had anticipated. In light of his ex-wife's remarks, he began to question his sexual adequacy.

In fact, there was nothing wrong with his capacity for sexual enjoyment. He was simply using sex to prove his manliness and to get even with his ex-wife. The pleasure from his escapades had to be shared with these nonsexual needs.

In both cases sex was seen as the problem. It was not. Marion and Paul were using sex to satisfy nonsexual needs. Whenever anyone does this, sexual pleasure decreases.

These cases demonstrate that sexual behavior can be, and is, motivated by many needs, the least of which may be sex. Rape is an excellent example of using sex to satisfy a completely nonsexual need. Behavioral scientists recognize that rape is not a sexual act or crime, but a crime of violence. It is the sexual expression of a violent impulse. Sex is the vehicle used to satisfy a need to hurt, humiliate or violate another person. Since it has taken society a long time to accept this idea, no doubt there will be even more resistance to accepting the idea that much of our "normal" sexual behavior is motivated by nonsexual needs.

HOW SEX LOSES ITS PLEASURE

How can a nonsexual need take pleasure out of the sex act? It does so through the creation of conflict; two unrelated needs, the sexual and the nonsexual, compete for satisfaction. Instead of enjoying the natural flow of sexual impulses, the conflict "pulls" our behavior in two different directions. Neither need is completely satisfied, and we are left feeling frustrated. The following examples illustrate how this happens:

John is starved for affection. The only time he receives affection is in bed during foreplay. As a result, he tries to prolong the foreplay stage. His body and psyche are torn between getting more affection and proceeding to intercourse. If he proceeds to intercourse, his affectional needs are frustrated; if he stops at the foreplay stage, his arousal urges him on. In either case, he cannot enjoy what is happening. After sex is over, he feels that something was missing.

John's hidden bedroom partner, his need for affection, robbed him of the pleasure and satisfaction he expected to receive from sex. Since he was aware only of his sexual needs, he blamed sex for his lack of satisfaction.

Mrs. W. is angry with her husband because he unmercifully insults her in public. She would really like to strike her husband to even the score, but instead, she has an affair. Her anger surfaces as furious pumping and aggressiveness in bed (much to her lover's enjoyment). No matter how aggressive she becomes, she does not feel satisfied.

Mrs. W.'s body and psyche are torn by the choices: to strike out in anger, cry out in hurt, or respond to the passionate touch of her lover.With such powerful bedroom partners vying for satisfaction, she *had* to feel disappointed.

SOMETHING TO CONSIDER

An accepted tenet of modern psychology is that repressed sexual needs can motivate nonsexual behaviors such as eating or artistic pursuits. Yet we have never considered the opposite possibility—that repressed nonsexual needs can influence and control sexual behavior. It is time to move forward from Freud. We must face the fact that much of our sexual behavior *is* motivated by nonsexual needs which surface and seek satisfaction during sex. This raises some crucial questions.

What are the repressed needs which seek expression in sex? Why do these needs surface in our sex lives? The needs which we repress in today's world are many. Consider some of the dilemmas of modern life: feelings of helplessness in an overpopulated world on the brink of destruction from war, contamination through pollution or radiation, loneliness and alienation, pressures to conform, the need to repress anger, the economic battle for survival, and changing sex roles.

In many facets of modern life we feel helpless and insignificant. Where then can we find expression for our need to assert ourselves, to make contact, to find security and reassurance, to feel competent and in control, to feel special and privileged?

We would answer with another question. Where, other than the bedroom, can we find a more convenient place for such needs to surface and seek satisfaction? The bedroom is the last bastion of modern man. It is the one area of complete privacy which can be shut off from the rest of the world. Alone with our mate, we are free to seek reassurance, security, support for waning confidence and self-esteem, or a haven from the horrors of modern reality. The bedroom is the one place we can freely unload or camouflage anger, seek confirmation of man or womanhood, even scores, and heal wounds. We can carry out our personal rebellion against societal norms. We can violate our humanity or confirm it. It is *easy* to use sex to dominate or submit, to honor or humiliate, to escape from loneliness or avoid emotional intimacy. The bedroom is the most convenient place for any of these to take place. Temptation and opportunity are always at hand.

Is it any wonder then, that there was such an uproar when Masters and Johnson and other scientists brought the laboratory into the bedroom? People want to protect their innermost secrets. But gradually the statistics were collected. The machines and surrogates did their work, and we were enlightened. Science scrutinized our methods, plotted our frequencies, and recorded our bodily reactions—inside and out. Everything was thoroughly examined—everything but motivation. No one bothered to ask *why* people have sex in the first place.

Perhaps this area was left unexplored because we assumed that people have sex because it's fun. Yet some people continue to have sex even when they don't enjoy it. Others enjoy it but don't have it often. Surely other motives are at work. We simply are not aware of them. These hidden motives and needs take their toll on sexual pleasure. The corporate climber who exploits his or her sexual prowess, the timid employee who becomes the demonic master of the bedroom, the lonely-heart who hops into bed rather than spend the night alone—all pay the price: loss of sexual enjoyment.

When ulterior or hidden motives pervade our sex lives, little room is left for sexual enjoyment. If we are obsessed with accumulating or pleasing partners, when we are worried about sinning, acting like an animal, or behaving in an undignified fashion, there is not much room for truly sexual feelings to surface.

Similarly, when one's body and psyche crave a haven from loneliness, or when we would like to get even for a past hurt, or receive the touch of reassurance or confirmation of our sexuality, there is no possibility of reaping the full measure of sexual pleasure. Sex born of these motives simply cannot lead to complete sexual satisfaction. Too much effort and energy is drained by these nonsexual needs. (How this happens will be discussed in later chapters.)

What can be done about it? Masters, Johnson, Lazarus and other therapists have developed new methods for increasing sexual pleasure. Sensate focus, deconditioning, and reconditioning have proven effective in thousands of cases. Yet many thousands more remain impervious to these techniques. These are the people who use sex to satisfy nonsexual needs. The solution is to uncover the nonsexual motives which intrude upon and spoil their sex lives. These needs then can be satisfied independently of sex, and banished from the bedroom. Sex will be relieved of these unwanted, unnatural burdens, and true sexual ecstasy can be achieved.

In the following chapters we shall discuss some of the more common nonsexual needs that interfere with one's sex life, how they interfere, the effects of this interference, and what can be done about it.

"I JUST DON'T UNDERSTAND IT. NO MATTER HOW MANY WOMEN I GO TO BED WITH I STILL FEEL LONELY."

2

Using Sex to Get Affection

The need to be touched, held, reassured, and comforted permeates the animal kingdom. Man is no exception. We all want affection. We all like to be touched, kissed and caressed. We also need to touch and be affectionate to others. Yet, in the United States, we are conditioned to restrain our impulses to hug and kiss friends, to hold and reassure each other, and to express affection openly. Thus, we do not have ample opportunities for satisfying our affectional needs.

All the conditioning in the world will not eliminate our need to give and receive affection. We merely learn to block this need from our awareness, leaving our affectional needs unsatisfied.

During sex there is considerable touching, kissing, and holding, and it is easy to see how the need for affection can surface and seek satisfaction. If couples do not get enough touching, holding or caressing outside the bedroom, sex will become the vehicle for the satisfaction of their affectional needs. These couples literally learn to have sex when they really want affection. Their sexual urges become conditioned to affectional needs. Affection automatically translates into sex.

It is important to emphasize that even though sex and affection are two different needs, they are not incompatible. Affectionate sex can be, and is, very healthy. However, it is not very good or healthy to limit affection to sex or vice versa.

Problems arise when sex is used as the major source of affection. For one thing, sex will provide less pleasure. With affectional needs fighting for satisfaction, it is difficult to focus on sexual needs. Second, a feeling that something is missing will follow the sex act. Neither affectional needs nor sexual needs will be completely satisfied. The partners will feel that they have been through a tug-of-war rather than a mutually enjoyable sexual experience.

Using sex as a major source of affection is surprisingly common in marriage. As the years pass, couples begin to take each other for granted. They forget to make each other feel loved and appreciated through frequent loving looks, caresses, or tender touches. These actions are shunted into the bedroom where they are compressed into ten minutes of foreplay. Such a stringent diet of affection is not satisfying, and can lead to affairs and undeclared war, as the following cases demonstrate.

Mrs. D. was sent for therapy by her husband who caught her with "someone who was a horrendous excuse for a man." She was a very conventional, religious woman, and was at a loss to explain her behavior. Married to an accountant who was a stickler for physical fitness and discipline, Mrs. D. tried to maintain his high standards, but never succeeded to her husband's satisfaction. In short, she was starved for affection and understanding.

Initially, she did not make the connection between the lack of affection in her life and the affair. She had met Mr. M. in a crowded restaurant when he offered to share his table. She described him as a "most kind and considerate man, somewhat roly-poly." She lamented, "I just can't understand it. I don't even find him physically attractive, yet I was willing to go to bed with him before lunch was over."

As she talked about the two men in her life, she realized that the affair with Mr. M had been motivated by her need for affection and understanding. She concluded, much to her relief, that she was not a tramp, but merely an affection-starved woman.

Mrs. D. had been unaware of the real problem in her marriage—that she was using sex to get affection. However, unsatisfied affectional needs do not always drive couples to have affairs. Instead, they may result in bickering and battling which can go on for years. In such a case, the couple is aware that something is wrong or missing, but neither partner can pinpoint the problem. In the following case, each partner had a piece of the puzzle but they could not put them together.

Mr. and Mrs. W. came for therapy because they were constantly bickering, and both felt abused and taken for granted. During one heated exchange, sex was mentioned: dead silence followed. Probing revealed that their sex life was in shambles. When we asked each partner to tell the other exactly what was wrong, both were hesitant and evasive. Finally they exploded with the following rather poetic and amusing exchange.

Mr. W. How can I know what's wrong with sex? You're so stingy with your canary, you'd think it would fly away if you lifted your skirt.

Mrs. W. Me, stingy? You're the miser. The way you hoard your kisses, you'd think they were gold. All you want to do is exercise *your* bird.

Mr. W. Who feels like kissing a cold fish?

Mrs. W. Who feels like spawning with one?

Mr. W. Me, cold? Ha! Sometimes I want to attack you and smother you with kisses, but I'll be damned if I'll kiss somebody who doesn't want to screw me.

Mrs. W. And I'll be damned if I'll have sex with someone who doesn't show me he loves me.

The W's had been waging an undeclared war, each failing to recognize and refusing to give what the other wanted. When the war was brought into the open, both finally agreed to a truce. He agreed to be more affectionate outside the bedroom, and she was only too glad to vent her sexuality independent of her affectional needs. Both learned that sex was not a substitute for love or affection, and that affection should not be limited to sex. Several weeks later neither could believe how much they had been missing.

"WHAT DO YOU MEAN I SHOULD BE MORE AFFECTIONATE OUTSIDE THE BEDROOM, DOCTOR? JUST LAST WEEK I KISSED HER WHEN SHE WON THE LOTTERY!"

You can tell if you're using sex to satisfy affectional needs simply by asking yourself, "Am I getting the affection I want outside of the bedroom?" If the answer is no, there is probably a carryover of this need into your sex life. If affection always leads to sex, or if no affection is exchanged outside the bedroom, then sex is certainly being used as a substitute for affection. As a result, you are not experiencing maximum sexual pleasure. Furthermore, the affection which is exchanged during sex cannot possibly satisfy your need for nonsexual affection. What should you do?

- Discuss specific affectional needs with your partner. For example, "I want more love," is too vague. "I need to be kissed and touched several times a day," is better. "A kiss or two before work would feel great. And if you touched me or smiled at me more often, I'd feel fantastic," is best. Draw pictures if you have to.
- Set aside 10–15 minutes before bedtime for affectionate conversation and caressing. Make sex off-limits during this time. This will eliminate the conflict between sex and affection. Once each of you has had your share of affection, sex will be much better.
- Develop the habit of hugging and kissing before and after work. Take time to really enjoy the morning kiss goodbye. It will give you something pleasant to recall and look forward to when you return.
- Learn to combine a compliment with an affectionate kiss or touch. "Thanks for the delightful lunch," carries more impact when followed by a touch or a kiss.
- Learn to show appreciation for the many things you do for each other daily.

A lack of affection is always accompanied by a lack of appreciation. Couples who really appreciate each others' pleasantries tend to be very affectionate, and we can't think of a nicer way to say "thank you."

In general, make a concerted effort to fulfill this need outside the bedroom. Sex will still be affectionate, and unsatisfied affectional needs won't detract from sexual enjoyment.

3

Avoiding Intimacy Through Sex

In our culture, sex is considered a private, intimate act. Naturally, we assume that when two people have sex, they are on intimate terms. However, this is not necessarily true. Sex certainly involves physical intimacy, but this has little to do with emotional intimacy.

Emotional intimacy has to do with understanding how a person thinks and feels. It develops over time as we share our innermost thoughts, feelings, aspirations, and fears. A couple can go through all the physical intimacies of intercourse and still remain emotional strangers. In fact, sex can be used to avoid emotional intimacy in three basic ways: by mending fences, arguing over sex, and building cages.

FENCE MENDING

Developing emotional intimacy involves facing and resolving conflicts together. This is an important way we get to know

15

ourselves and our mates: through resolving conflicts we build emotional intimacy. However, sex can be used to short-circuit this process. Each time an emotional issue arises between partners it is shoved aside in favor of sex.

This happened to Tina and Gary. During disagreements one or the other would suddenly realize that angry words were being exchanged and would begin to apologize. The apology by one would elicit affection from the other. Sex would follow. Each used profuse affection and sexual favors to prove that the angry words were only accidental. After sex, their conversation would focus on how compatible they were in bed.

Gary and Tina never allowed the underlying issues to surface. There was no exchange of views, no airing of gripes, no resolution of differences, and very little discussion of feelings. Physically, they were intimate; emotionally, they were strangers. Sex short-circuited the process of self- and mutual exploration. As a couple, they did not grow together.

Couples who avoid issues and seek refuge in bed have static relationships. They remain self-oriented and never learn to understand each other. These couples tend to recycle the same arguments year after year. They do not mature because they do not learn to resolve differences. In fact, since they never explore the real issues, they do not get to know their real differences. In short, these couples keep themselves in the dark by jumping into bed when problems arise. Sex is used to avoid conflict.

ARGUING OVER SEX

Some couples avoid emotional intimacy by arguing about sex. Their lives consist of an unending battle over problems in the bedroom; little or no attention is given to nonsexual problems. Couples who use this strategy to avoid intimacy tend to make such comments as "Our relationship is perfect, except for sex. And we fight about it all the time." We have observed two types of patterns in these pseudo-sexual battles. In one, the couple has sex regularly. Their arguments center around whose turn it is to do what to whom, who did most of the "work," who enjoyed it more, and who was more selfish or giving. Most often we find that the sexual issue reflects the nonsexual issue, as in the case of David and Liz.

This couple argued constantly over sex. Each complained about the performance of the other in terms of frequency, duration, or level of enthusiasm. Each thought the other was basically a good lover, but somehow neither was satisfied.

It became apparent that David and Liz were total emotional strangers. Both were selfish and immature, paying little attention to the needs of the other. This was their "real" battle, yet neither could see that anything but sex was amiss.

We solved the problem by forbidding them to argue about sex in our office. They simply had to find something else to fight over. This was very difficult for them. At first they could not come up with anything, both insisting that everything else was perfect. We instructed each of them to make up a problem. After some hesitation the floodgates broke open.

Such cases are usually long-term and difficult. The couple is not used to facing and resolving problems. It is hard for them to discuss feelings and take responsibility for what they feel. Sex becomes the focus of their battle because it is a ready target.

Each partner has the attitude that "If I'm not enjoying myself, it's your fault. You're doing something that I don't like." Over the long haul, neither their sex life nor their relationship improves.

The second pattern of pseudo-sexual arguments centers

around lack of sex. Couples who fall into this category avoid emotional intimacy by withholding sex. It works like this: both partners agree that each wants sex more often, but they just don't get together as often as they'd like. Each has a host of valid reasons why "now" is not the right time.

Initially both partners are very understanding, but resentment, hurt feelings, and a sense of sexual inadequacy gradually build up. Eventually their relationship consists of constant battling over who is at fault. Such a pattern developed between Mark and Faith.

They came for therapy because, as they said, "We have a sex problem." Their problem: for the past ten years of their twelve-year marriage, they had sex less than once a week. Each felt sex was enjoyable and didn't seem to have any obvious hang-ups. Both claimed they wanted it more often, yet something always seemed to get in the way. Every time the therapist attempted to explore nonsexual areas of the relationship, the conversation drifted back to sex. When the therapist focused on this pattern, Faith blurted out, "Just like at home. That's all we ever do—fight about sex. We're so busy fighting we never get around to doing. *That's* the problem!"

The true problem came to light in a later session when Faith and Mark exchanged a few of their usual accusations.

Mark. Sometimes I think you don't want sex.
Faith. Maybe I don't want sex because of the kind of guy you turned out to be.
Therapist. (interrupting a series of name-calling) Hold it! Faith, what kind of guy did Mark turn out to be?
Faith. I don't know. How could I? All we ever do is fight about sex. I'm not kidding. We set out to take in a movie and bang! Next thing you know, we're fighting. Not over which movie to see, but sex. It's crazy.
Therapist. Sounds very frustrating.
Faith. It's maddening. I really don't know my husband. Sometimes I feel like I'm living with a total stranger.

Thus the real issue surfaced: two strangers sharing the same bed. For ten years they argued about and focused on sex. They grew apart and slowly withdrew from each other. Their sex life merely reflected what was happening emotionally. Faith and Mark were withdrawing from each other sexually *and* emotionally. They avoided true emotional contact by using sex as the pseudo-issue.

CAGE BUILDING

In the previous cases, both partners were cooperating to avoid emotional intimacy. In cage building, one partner pursues intimacy while the other avoids it. The partner avoiding intimacy—the cage builder—may do so either deliberately or without being aware of what is happening. Every time an emotional issue surfaces, the cage builder directs the other partner to the bedroom, as in the following case of newlyweds, Louise and Tim.

Whenever their conversation at home shifted to Louise, she became evasive and seductive. For example, one evening Tim was expressing disappointment and sadness. He asked Louise what kinds of things made her sad. Her response was to coyly caress his neck and shoulders while whispering, "Who wants to talk about sadness. There are better things to do."

Louise did not want to know about Tim's sadness, his feelings of inadequacy and helplessness, or any unpleasant emotions. Abandoned by her father, she had been raised in a poverty-level home. Any negative talk revived memories which she preferred to forget. She would thus bury the problem in the bedroom. In the process, she prevented herself from getting to know Tim as anything but a protective male.

Sometimes the cage builder will equate sex with intimacy to confuse the other partner, as in the case of Mr. and Mrs. J. Mrs. J. felt something was missing from her marriage. She felt trapped by her husband, a highly verbal and convincing person.

"I LIKE TO BE ON INTIMATE TERMS
BEFORE I GO TO BED WITH SOMEONE.
DO YOU LIKE TO BE ON TOP OR
BOTTOM?"

Mr. J had assured her that their relationship was intimate, that there were no secrets, and that everything was fine. But lately Mrs. J. had become less sure. She felt she lived with a mirror image of herself. Mr. J., it seems, would say or do whatever he thought Mrs. J wanted. He felt he was open and honest with nothing to hide. Any attempt to penetrate his facade was frustrated. For example:

> *Mrs. J.* But I feel I don't know you. I really don't know anything important about you—how you think or feel about anything.
> *Mr. J.* Well, whose fault is that? Ask me anything and I'll tell you. I have nothing to hide or be ashamed of.
> *Mrs. J.* But I want you to be you, not what you think I want you to be. I want us to be close.

Mr. J. Don't we have good sex? Don't you feel close then? Don't you get what you want?
Mrs. J. See! Even there. It's what *I* want. What do *you* want?
Mr. J. I want to see you have a good time and you sure seem like you do. Isn't that enough?
Mrs. J. No! Yes! I don't know! (dissolves in tears)
Mr. J. I think that's the problem. You don't know what you want.

In this case Mr. J. successfully avoided intimacy by answering Mrs. J's questions with other questions. This placed her on the defensive. When she became confused, Mr. J attacked her and laid responsibility for the problem in her lap.

In reality both were confused. He successfully avoided her by equating sex with intimacy. She didn't know how to differentiate between the two, and thus was unable to work through the confusion he had created. Neither was clearly aware of the distinction between physical and emotional intimacy. Once the distinction was made, therapy proceeded to a successful resolution.

It's easy to understand why sex can be used to avoid intimacy. The act itself is physically intimate and *can* be a vehicle for the expression of emotional intimacy. Some couples simply confuse the physical aspect of sex with intimacy. Others fend off or avoid emotional closeness by focusing on sex. In either case, sex becomes less satisfying and the couples remain strangers. As these cases demonstrated, years of sharing one's bed with a stranger can be quite frustrating and unfulfilling.

Teenagers and young adults are the most frequent victims of this "sex with a familiar stranger" syndrome. Their lack of maturity and experience leads them to believe that when two people have sex, they are intimate and really know each other. These relationships are usually short-lived; those who do marry frequently get divorced in short order. It doesn't take long for them to realize that they have been bedding with a stranger they don't even like. Undoubtedly this helps account for the extremely high divorce rate among those who marry young.

*   *   *

Who is likely to use sex to avoid intimacy? Couples who believe that good marital partners don't fight, couples who do not really know themselves, and couples who feel uncomfortable sharing their true feelings are apt to fall into this trap. In most cases these persons don't know what they want, and have a negative self-image. Hence their reluctance to reveal themselves.

Using sex to avoid intimacy obviously endangers a relationship. In fact, a relationship cannot be developed at all with sex as the only bond, or with sex as a substitute for emotional closeness. You can tell a couple is using sex to avoid intimacy if:

● arguments and disagreements always lead to sex.
● they feel close and intimate only in the bedroom.
● they cannot readily share thoughts and feelings.
● when emotional issues are brought up, the subject gets sidetracked in favor of sex.
● they feel they are bedding with strangers.
● they constantly argue over sex.

What can be done to break the pattern of using sex to avoid intimacy?

● The couple must agree not to fight over sex (or be forbidden to do so by the therapist).
● The couple should schedule a 10-minute session each night before bedtime to discuss personal issues and feelings without *any* sex talk or contact. During these sessions each partner should make a point to share the following: a personal thought or feeling; something about him or herself that the other does not know; a family incident discussing specifically each partner's reaction to it—how it affected their feelings and their view of the family, and what possible repercussions it might have.

Couples must pay particular attention to the similarities and differences between their reactions and feelings and those of their partner, never criticizing, always accepting how the other feels. Sharing feelings about daily incidents helps them to understand each other and grow close emotionally. This is how intimacy develops. Sex can never serve this function.

4

Avoiding Loneliness Through Sex

Our society emphasizes togetherness. From childhood through adolescence, our educational systems, churches, and families encourage gregariousness and sociability. People spend little time by themselves as they grow up. Even as adults most choose not to be alone. In fact, many people find loneliness intolerable. Yet all people, married or single, experience it.

Going to Times Square on a New Year's Eve when feeling lonely and depressed, and being among thousands of cheering people, is not likely to make a person feel happy. In fact, he or she will probably feel more depressed afterwards.

So it is with sex. Since it involves close contact, it seems an ideal way to camouflage or fight loneliness. But this is a losing proposition. The physical closeness of the sex act never can satisfy the emotional need for human contact and understanding. Sex will seem hollow and will be very frustrating because the need for human care and understanding is unsatisfied. But, as usual, sex will be blamed, since it is easier to focus on the physical than on the emotional. By switching attention away from the emotional, people in this situation do not give themselves a chance to deal with the loneliness. They come to believe that the touching, kissing, and intimacy of sex is all they need or desire. Yet it will never seem like enough.

LONELINESS AND THE SINGLE PERSON

Everyone experiences feelings of loneliness. However, the person who lives alone is apt to feel lonely more frequently. We have worked with men and women who, rather than spend the night alone, bed with someone they may not really like.

What's wrong with singles going to bed to avoid being alone? It certainly seems understandable. But there are important emotional and sexual consequences.

First, as in any relationship, sex cannot satisfy the need for companionship. If there is no emotional bond, after sex is over partners will feel frustrated or unsatisfied, and will mistakenly blame their dissatisfaction on poor sex instead of on inadequate companionship. The pleasure derived from sex will decrease unless the need for companionship is satisfied first.

Second, by jumping the gun and going to bed first, couples often short-circuit the possibility of satisfying their need for companionship. Few lasting friendships start in the bedroom.

Third, when people are lonely, they find it easier to convince themselves that they love the person with whom they are having sex. They are also more accepting of faults and more apt to tolerate emotional abuse.

Many persons, driven by loneliness to believe that they are in love, become trapped in a relationship that progresses too far too fast. When the loneliness subsides, the relationship is often continued out of guilt. For example, someone in this situation might reason that "I love this person. We have too much invested in each other to break up now."

Kathy was a victim of such a relationship. Suffering from

intense loneliness after her boyfriend left her, she went out with the first man who asked. Bud, her date, was also a very lonely person who had just moved into the city. They spent the night together and had sex. For the next few months they were inseparable.

Then tempers began to flare as they discovered "faults" in each other. The relationship dragged on in spite of the increasingly obvious fact that they were completely incompatible. Kathy felt abused, and her self-esteem plummeted. Out of desperation she came for therapy. Soon she realized that her common bond with Bud was not love but fear of loneliness. Neither wanted to face the intense isolation each had experienced prior to their first date with each other.

Kathy was fortunate. She was able to break off the relationship before she got trapped in a miserable marriage.

Bob and Billie Joe were not so lucky. Their backgrounds were similar to Kathy's and Bud's. However, during a period of relative calm in their otherwise stormy relationship, they decided to get married. Their relationship continued to deteriorate, but they had to work it out because they had too much invested in it. After eight years of "working it out," Bob and Billie Joe separated.

Their separation consisted of Bob moving across the street to another apartment. They were constantly on the telephone and would end up in the same bed a couple of times each week. Neither felt the other was a good lover, and most of their meetings ended in bickering. When Billie Joe came for therapy, she said she didn't enjoy the sexual aspect of their separation. Despite her dissatisfaction with sex, it was the only thing they came close to having in common. She began to realize that sex was being used to avoid being alone.

Billie Joe faced her fear of loneliness. She began to develop her own resources and interests by taking courses and playing racquetball. She became more independent and self-sufficient, and eventually lost interest in Bob.

These cases illustrate some of the problems single persons can create for themselves by running into the bedroom to escape being alone. Living by oneself may be lonely, but living with someone and bickering constantly is difficult as well as lonely.

LONELINESS AND THE MARRIED PERSON

Sex between married persons also can be motivated by loneliness. Instead of dealing with the feelings, these couples end up in bed. The feeling of emptiness after such an encounter comes from an unsatisfied need for human contact, not from inadequate sexual performance. As usual, however, sex will bear the brunt of the blame.

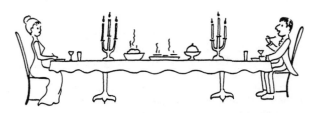

"WHY ON EARTH WOULD YOU FEEL LONELY? WE'RE MARRIED!"

This was the case for Mr. and Mrs. F. Mr. F. had many hobbies and interests. Mrs. F. had none. Often she would desire closeness and contact with her husband who was absorbed in reading, golf, or other diversions. She learned to lure her husband away from his interests with sex. He responded, and they would go to bed. For Mrs. F. the experience was not very satisfying. Eventually she became disinterested in sex and came for therapy because "she had a sex problem." Mrs. F. soon learned that she was *not* sexually frustrated. She was lonely for meaningful companionship. Trying to satisfy this need in the bedroom created the illusion that her problem was sexual.

There is no doubt that married persons can feel intense loneliness, which can be difficult to face and resolve. Married persons who are lonely often can't imagine how it is possible to feel isolated in the company of a loving partner and family. Thus they may be reluctant to discuss the matter with their mate. Mr. J's problem is an example of how hiding these feelings can increase the sense of isolation.

He came for therapy because he had "lost his sexual appetite." His real problem was uncovered in the first session. The following exchange took place after Mr. J. revealed how often he used to have sex. As he spoke he became progressively more somber.

Therapist. Well, how long has it been since you've had sex?
Mr. J. (bowed head) I . . . I . . . guess I don't know . . . a long time. . . . I haven't been feeling very horny lately.
Therapist. How have you been feeling?
Mr. J. (crying) Lonely, alone, all alone (between sobs). I know it's crazy. . . . It doesn't make sense . . . it's driving me nuts. I have a wife and two kids, but I still feel all alone.

It turned out that not only was Mr. J. not sharing his concerns with his wife; he was pushing himself further and further from her. As his feelings of loneliness increased, he communicated less, intensifying his unhappiness. He was encouraged to communicate his feelings of alienation to his wife. She listened with concern and shared her own experience of such emotions. As communication channels were reestablished, their sex life improved.

In these cases the relationships were restored to health. Unfortunately, some are not. Many unhealthy relationships, among both the married and single, are perpetuated because one or both partners fear living alone. Usually, the longer these relationships persist, the more difficult it is to uncover the real issues. Thus, any unhealthy relationship should be broken off as soon as the incompatibility becomes clear. The longer the delay and the more the couple has invested, the more difficult it becomes to end the relationship. We often have heard this lament: "I guess when it really comes down to it, I got married because I thought it would be better than being alone. Now I wonder."

* * *

Those people who are likely to use sex to avoid loneliness:

- are insecure and not comfortable with themselves.
- have limited interests or hobbies.
- have not developed their inner resources and rely on others for entertainment, direction, or support.
- have never learned to cope with being alone.

The best ways to prevent the use of sex for dealing with loneliness are to:

- Develop new interests and skills. Persons who have no hobbies or personal interests suffer the most severe bouts of loneliness. They have nothing with which to occupy their time and become preoccupied with being alone.
- Cultivate friendships outside the sexual relationship. All too often, once people find a bed partner, they assume that this is all they need and they stop looking for friends. Everyone needs friends in addition to the person chosen as a sex partner.
- Share any feelings of loneliness before sex, not after it. Sharing such feelings builds intimacy and satisfies some needs for closeness.

- Cultivate friendships among peers of the same sex. In this way the chances of misusing sex are minimized.
- Adopt a healthy attitude toward loneliness. Feelings of loneliness are common to all humans and are nothing to be feared. People do not need other people all the time. It is most important to feel comfortable with oneself. In this way sex will not be burdened by loneliness, nor will the burden of loneliness be placed on your partner.

5

Sex for Atonement

Jill and Art came for therapy because "Jill was a nymphomaniac. . . ." Their therapy sessions uncovered the following sequence of events.

Shortly after their marriage Art had informed Jill that she was a poor lover. As he put it, "Jill couldn't satisfy me." Jill took this admonishment to heart and went through all sorts of antics to satisfy her husband. For a while he was happy, but eventually nothing she did was enough. Understandably, her feelings of sexual adequacy took a nose dive. At this point her husband pressured her into swinging. She was very attractive and they were in great demand. Before long it was obvious to everyone, including Art, that Jill was the desired member of the team. She gained a reputation as a sexual pro. Jill enjoyed the attention and the reputation. Sex with other men was a welcome relief from the pressure she felt in her marriage bed; other men were easy to please and returned her favors and attention, something Art had never done.

Art was a liability in the swinging world, lying back and expecting to be entertained, just as he did at home. Eventually no one wanted to go to bed with him, and he soon wanted to give up swinging and return to a monogamous marriage. When

Jill refused, he tried to save face by labeling her a nymphomaniac who needed to be cured.

In therapy Jill and Art learned that sexual pleasure is the
responsibility of both partners. Art had tried to make it entirely
Jill's duty. She had accepted this responsibility without question, taking it upon herself to make up for Art's lack of enjoyment. This is exactly what happens when sex is used for
atonement. One partner assumes total responsibility for the
sexual happiness and well-being of both.

A surprising number of couples do not share equal responsibility for sexual pleasure. The problem first shows itself with
one partner hinting at sexual dissatisfaction, perhaps with a
simple comment that sex is not as much fun as it used to be.
The "responsible" partner then expends an inordinate amount
of time and energy trying to correct matters by taking the
initiative to search for things that will please the dissatisfied
partner. The "responsible" partner ends up ignoring his or her
own needs or desires, and sex becomes a chore and a duty. No
one can cater entirely to someone else's needs without eventually feeling resentful, angry, or inadequate. Meanwhile the
"irresponsible" partner, assuming that everything is now as it
should be, simply absorbs the increased attention. The imbal-
ance continues to develop without either partner's real awareness.

Sometimes this situation grows throughout a couple's married life until the partners come to see themselves as sexually
incompatible. The workhorse of the team avoids sex because
the pressure to satisfy the other partner destroys any pleasure
sex might offer. The irresponsible partner becomes more fussy
and demanding and so continues to see the workhorse as inadequate. Both contribute to the illusion that the workhorse
is not working hard enough, while the irresponsible partner
has a healthy sex drive.

This would have happened to Jill and Art if the reality of
the swinging world had not backfired on Art. By labeling Jill

a nymphomaniac and seeking her cure, he brought attention to his own need for therapy.

Sometimes both partners assume too much responsibility for sexual satisfaction; instead of focusing on mutual pleasure, they focus on one another's enjoyment and forget their own. This can result in some of the following ironic situations.

Steve had serious doubts about his manhood. In a private therapy session he explained that his wife, Pauline, seemed to want to have sex more than he did. This worried him because he felt it should be the other way around: "Real men want sex more than women." In an effort to outdo his wife, Steve had tried to force himself to have sex every day. Yet each time, his wife was ready, willing, and seemed to want more.

Steve had not discussed any of this with Pauline because he didn't want her to think there might be something wrong with his "masculinity." The therapist convinced Steve that there was nothing physically wrong with someone who wanted sex every day, and nothing physically wrong with someone who didn't. Steve agreed to let his wife in on his problem.

This is where the irony of the situation became apparent. Concerned that he might not be happy with their sex life, and determined to keep her man happy, Pauline had let Steve know that she was available any time, any place. "After all," she said, "I know how men are and what they want."

Steve had perceived Pauline's willingness as a threat to his masculinity and so had forced himself to have sex daily. Pauline had thought, because of his increased requests, that Steve was not getting enough, so she made it clear that she too was ready for more. In fact, Steve was getting too much, feeling overwhelmed, and beginning to doubt his "manhood." Pauline was also oversatiated, but was determined to satisfy her partner. Neither really enjoyed the sex. Both were using it for nonsexual reasons—Steve to defend his masculinity, and Pauline to please and satisfy her man. They thought they were sexually incompatible or had some other kind of sex problem. In fact they were misusing sex because of a simple communication problem.

Sam and Sylvia's case is also a good example of a communication problem. They came for therapy after seven years of marriage and "lousy sex." The following excerpt, taken from their second session, capsulizes their problem.

> *Sam.* Just because that thing comes up at the drop of a hat doesn't mean all you have to do is lay back and spread your legs. You know I like other things too, not just the same old stuff.
> *Sylvia.* Yeah? Like what? Another woman!?
> *Sam.* Ha, Ha. You could try wearing something sexy for openers. Those damn flannel tents you wear aren't too exciting.
> *Sylvia.* Look at him, will ya! It would help if *you* did something once in a while. Just because you're standing there erect and ready doesn't mean I'm ready and waiting. It takes more than a stiffer to get me hopping, you know.

Cases like this usually arise from false assumptions. Sylvia thought that because Sam was erect he wanted to bypass foreplay and go straight to intercourse. Sam thought that because Sylvia didn't do anything, *she* was always ready for action. Each presumed to know what the other wanted, and each wanted to please the other. However, both misinterpreted the situation.

Simple, direct communication will usually clear up such problems. No person can read another's mind, so each partner must be responsible for telling the other what is personally exciting and desirable.

Sex for atonement is not limited to transactions in the bedroom: a surprising number of couples use sex to reconcile hurts or failures that have nothing to do with sex per se. In such cases one partner tries to nurse the other through life's trials and tribulations using sex as the nurturant. Here are two examples:

Joan would come home from the office feeling angry or hurt

because something had gone wrong. To soothe her, her husband Jack would shower her with compliments about her attractiveness and physical beauty. He would inevitably lead her to the bedroom where he would soothe her ruffled feathers by indulging her with sexual favors.

Marge was a social butterfly; Frank was somewhat inept. Whenever he experienced rejection or had a miserable time at a social gathering she would make up for it with a delightful time in bed.

Both Marge and Jack used sex to try to make up for their partner's disappointments, thinking they were being kind, understanding, and helpful. In fact, they were perpetuating immature, maladaptive behavior: Frank was reinforced for social incompetence, Joan for coming home angry. If either wanted a special treat in bed all he or she had to do was screw up at a party or the office. With such a powerful reward why should Frank learn to socialize or Joan to resolve her business problems?

Using sex for atonement is harmful in two ways. First, sex is never experienced at maximum pleasure by either partner. The appeaser feels sex is a duty while the receiver takes it for granted. Second, using sex in this manner prevents both partners from growing emotionally; the appeasing responsible partner becomes a wet nurse for the receiving, infantile one. Neither learns to take responsibility for his or her own faults and pleasure.

Lopsided relationships like those described are apt to develop when one partner has an egocentric orientation or a stereotyped attitude toward the opposite sex. For example, believing that:

- women are passive by nature and do not enjoy sex.
- men should be the aggressors.
- it is a wife's duty to please her husband.

- men should keep women "barefoot and pregnant."
- men are rough and inconsiderate.
- women want to be pampered.
- women are fragile and must be handled with extreme care.
- "I can't enjoy sex unless I get what I want."
- "I have to be put in the mood."
- "Sex isn't fun unless I'm really horny."
- "I have to be inspired to have good sex."

All of these attitudes interfere with sexual pleasure by discounting partners as individuals with unique needs and desires. Ignoring individuality makes it easy to accept too much responsibility or to take each other for granted. The more mature, conscientious partner becomes the workhorse; the more egocentric partner becomes the audience, demanding entertainment and satisfaction.

These problems can be corrected. First, both partners agree that sexual pleasure is an individual responsibility as well as a mutual consideration. Second, each of you must openly state what you prefer or find pleasurable. Third, brainstorm together for ways each of you can find personal enjoyment while helping the other feel satisfied. (Consult the suggestions at the end of the chapter on self-esteem.) In addition you can:

- Reverse roles: have the man do what the woman normally does and vice versa. This should help to develop a sense of empathy for each other, and prevent taking each other for granted.
- Try your expectations out on yourself before placing new demands on your partner. Never expect anything from your partner that you are not willing to try yourself.
- Have open discussions on sex, going into detail about what you feel and how you experience different aspects

of sex. Include positive and negative aspects of each experience: for example, "French kissing turns me on, but when you slobber all over me I lose interest."

- Share detailed fantasies about what you'd like to do and experience with each other, "I'd like you to be more aggressive," is vague. "Squeeze harder," is specific. "Squeeze my butt harder, but go easy on the nipples," is more specific. For best results, demonstrate these fantasies for each other.

6

Sex to Safeguard Fidelity

Sexual infidelity deals a painful blow to any relationship, as couples who want, need, and prize sexual fidelity are acutely aware. In fact many couples feel that marriage cannot exist without fidelity. This need and desire for faithfulness exerts considerable influence over sexual behavior. Couples who prize fidelity will go to great lengths to prevent wandering. Some of their efforts can actually be counterproductive: Oversatiation and hording are two such tactics.

OVERSATIATION

Oversatiation means indulging beyond need or desire. To prevent unfaithfulness, some couples indulge more frequently than they can possibly want or enjoy. Regardless of their true desires, they may have sex every day. (At least one couple we saw had sex every morning and evening.) Such behavior is supposed to insure fidelity. It seldom does.

"GREAT NEWS HELEN! I SOLVED OUR PROBLEM WITH BOREDOM. MONDAYS WE'LL HAVE IT IN THE GARAGE. TUESDAYS IN THE TUB. WEDNESDAYS UNDER THE DINING ROOM TABLE. THURSDAYS ON TOP OF...."

Most people do not go to the extreme of routine morning and evening sex. However, many couples do occasionally use oversatiation. Bob and Mary present a good example. Bob's job occasionally required some overnight travel. Prior to each trip, Mary would insist on having sex several times, not because she really enjoyed it, but because she was concerned about Bob's impending absence and freedom. Bob didn't enjoy it either. He felt coerced. Mary's excessive insecurity also made him feel as if he were abandoning her.

He began to resent and avoid sex; mutual accusations of infidelity and lack of interest followed. As usual, sex was being blamed for a problem that should have been settled outside the bedroom.

In the past, overindulgence to secure fidelity was used primarily by women. Today, an increasing number of men use it as well, insisting on a flurry of sexual activity prior to and following their wife's business trips—"to keep them faithful." Initially the wives may find this endearing. They will enjoy the added attention and will be generous with their reassurances. But resentment over lack of trust eventually surfaces, just as it did for husbands whose wives were distrustful.

Overindulgence as a means of safeguarding fidelity is based on the false assumption that a partner will not succumb to temptation if there is more than enough at home. Individuals who use this method seem to think sexual urges are subject to the principles of accounting: "Each time we have sex is one less time he/she will want it outside the marriage bed." This is not true. Excessive sex extinguishes sexual desire toward the person who demands the excess. Satiation, boredom, and resentment eventually set in; sex becomes a duty, a demanded performance. Under such stress no one can really enjoy it.

The idea of a new partner becomes appealing for two additional reasons. First, the variety afforded by a new partner breaks up the boredom that can develop with a regular partner.

Second, sex with a new partner will inevitably seem more enjoyable and less pressured because it is not done out of duty or the need to maintain fidelity: it will seem like an escape or mecca. Thus the net effect of oversatiation may well be to encourage infidelity. The following case history provides a good, though extreme, example of how deceptive oversatiation can be.

Mrs. Jones came to therapy because "All of a sudden my marriage fell apart." She had taken a lover considerably younger than herself; her husband had run away with someone older; their children were constantly in tears and shunted between relatives. She couldn't understand how it had all happened because, "We had such a solid relationship."

Discussion revealed that their "solid" relationship consisted of having sex at least twice a day since they were married eleven years earlier. Their entire life and daily routine seemed to center around sex. According to Mrs. Jones, by mutual agreement they had a "quickie" before each went to the office, to hold them over until the evening. They spent a large part of the evening having intercourse until neither could take more.

This ritual went on for six years. When the children came along they were sent to a friend's, to their rooms, or to watch TV while mom and dad locked themselves in the bedroom. An objective observer might honestly conclude that they were trying to wipe out each other's sex drive.

Sexual fidelity was a high priority for Mr. and Mrs. Jones. They swore to be true until death, and took what they thought were appropriate steps to maintain this priority. (One must admire their dedication.) Both prized and bragged about their fidelity. Each was absolutely sure the other would never even look at anyone else.

So Mrs. Jones was understandably shocked and confused when she found herself uncontrollably attracted to a college student who was hired to do landscaping around their home. It became the neighborhood scandal. Mr. Jones sought refuge with an older woman who was very understanding and less demanding in bed.

Mrs. Jones and, eventually, Mr. Jones (when he finally came for therapy) both agreed that such frequent sex was neither desirable nor "all that enjoyable." They also realized what constrained, boring lives they led because of their attitude toward sex. We explored alternative ways to preserve fidelity. Within about a year, sex became less important to their relationship, its frequency dropping to well within the national average. Mr. and Mrs. Jones felt they were doing reasonably well.

SATIATING VARIETY

Experimentation in the bedroom helps to keep sex interesting and enjoyable, but experimentation and variety can be oversatiating just as easily as frequency. In this form of over-satiation a couple views variety as the key to a happy, life-long marriage.

One or both partners continually demand new and different positions and techniques to keep sex interesting. They try one novelty after another, and their creativity is truly amazing. Unfortunately, when the motive for such variety is to insure fidelity, much of the enjoyment is squelched. Why?

The need for sexual experimentation which springs from the natural evolution of a relationship is driven by a need to explore each other. The focal point is the couple. They learn each other's needs, desires, and preferences. The couple's goal is mutual understanding and sexual satisfaction, harmony and intimacy. Sexual experimentation which springs from the need to maintain fidelity is driven by the need to keep sex interesting. The focal point is the search for variety and physical pleasure and intensity. The couple's goal is to make each episode better and more exciting than the last.

These couples seldom take time to really explore each alternative in depth. No one can sample anything new just once or twice and really have a thorough understanding and feel for it, and there is always some anxiety and discomfort in trying anything new. Trying it only once or twice barely allows partners enough time to work out the physical logistics and dispel anxiety. Finally, couples tend to lose each other in the frenzy to find the new and better. They focus on the *degree* of pleasure each episode renders instead of its effect on each other and the relationship.

In sum, healthy variety evolves in the natural development of a sexual relationship. It is couple-centered, and is conceived and fully explored in an atmosphere of caring and curiosity. It is not driven by the need to secure fidelity. We are reminded of the extreme case of a woman who suggested swinging to keep her husband interested in her. The logic of this move escaped us. She explained, "With all this variety, it will take him longer to get tired of me."

HOARDING SEX

Last, and least common, is the attempt to keep a partner faithful by *not* having sex. We were baffled the first time we encountered this approach to fidelity, which seems to be based on the assumption that "what you don't get keeps you interested and coming back for more." The following case is a good example.

Phil and Joyce came for therapy because "We have a terrible sex life . . . it's nonexistent." They had been married less than three years and already had sex less than twice a month. This perplexed them because they both enjoyed sex and seemed to have healthy attitudes toward it. We could find no evidence of hidden nonsexual motives at work and were about to give up when the following angry interchange took place.

> *Phil.* (desperately) God dammit! I just can't understand you. The way you hoard it you'd think it was gold! What the hell are you saving it for, anyway?
> *Joyce.* (snapping and gesturing threateningly) It *is* gold! And I'm saving it for the jackass I'm sitting next to!
> *Phil.* Jackass! You're the donkey who won't give.
> *Therapist.* Hold it! Joyce, you're saving it for Phil?
> *Joyce.* (screaming) You're damn right. If I hold back it keeps him interested. If he gets all he wants now, what will keep him coming back 10 years from now? (looks shocked) He'll get tired of . . . (cries) . . . (laughs). . . . God . . . I feel so silly. I had no idea what I was doing.

As often happens, the couple discovered that the real problem had little to do with sex. Here it had to do with Joyce's insecurity, her feeling that no one would want a long-term relationship with her. She was using sex for a nonsexual purpose: to keep Phil faithful.

Few cases are so extreme. However, many couples use a mild form of sexual hoarding which we call "weekend sex." They have sex only on weekends. Should the urge arise before the prescribed time, it is suppressed. This is understandable when exhaustion or physical separation motivates such hoarding, but in most cases we question the wisdom of weekend sex. Why?

1. Sexual urges are not ruled by clock or calendar.
2. The best sex is usually spontaneous and unplanned.
3. Saving sex for the weekend creates pressure:
   (a) to have it even if the mood or emotional overtones of the relationship at that time are not conducive to sex.
   (b) to have a fantastic sexual experience every time, an expectation which itself creates more pressure.

Weekend sex is usually a symptom of other problems. It is often motivated by insecurity. These couples feel that sex during the week will be mediocre and will detract from the weekend "fireworks." This is just a way of camouflaging a "low sex drive" (which to us means other nonsexual motives are at work). The couple creates the illusion that because they just can't wait for the weekend, they have high sex drives. If their sex drives are so high, why wait?

* * *

Who is apt to use these techniques in a relationship? Most often it is individuals who overemphasize the importance of sex and ignore the emotional side of marriage. Sexual fidelity can never be guaranteed. The best prevention against infidelity is a deep and meaningful relationship, where each partner tries to satisfy the other's emotional and sexual needs. It is when these needs are not being expressed and satisfied that people are most vulnerable to the lure of a new partner.

Fidelity is not something to risk on games of withholding or gorging on sex. It needs to be nurtured through trust, open discussion, and the building of emotional bonds.

There are some things you can do to avoid using sex as the guardian of fidelity:

- Make a list of the attributes in your partner which you like and admire. Include how each one makes you feel. Then share this list with your partner.
- Make a list of the nonsexual needs which your partner satisfies for you. Consider how important each is. Again, share with your partner.
- Do the same for yourself: list your positive attributes and the needs that you satisfy for your partner. Consider how they help him/her. Discuss them with your partner. Ask your partner to draw up a similar list about you.
- List some of the nonsexual goals you and your partner have for your relationship, the things you'd like to do, experience, share, and so on.
- Several times a week, tell your partner one thing you appreciate about him/her outside the bedroom.

Consider how important these nonsexual needs, attributes, and goals are to you: how they help your personal development and how they help build a solid relationship. Strengthen the emotional bonds and your sex life will follow suit.

7

Sex to Confirm Sexuality

Sexual identity is a label for the feelings we have about ourselves as sexual beings. There are two parts to a sexual identity:

Part A: What we think of ourselves as lovers. We feel competent or incompetent depending on the success and satisfaction we experience in the bedroom.

Part B: How comfortable we feel about being a man or a woman. Our degree of comfort is determined by how well we meet our personal definition of what it means to be masculine or feminine, man or woman, *outside of the bedroom.*

When we feel sexually competent *and* meet our personal standards of manhood or womanhood, we have a solid, integrated sexual identity. We tend to have healthy, active, satisfying sex lives. Problems arise when we do not feel comfortable in the bedroom *or* do not have and meet clearly defined personal standards of what it means to be male or female. An inadequate or undeveloped sexual identity can and does exert considerable influence on our sex lies. How? Let us consider the individual who feels uncomfortable in the bedroom.

It's only natural to avoid any activity in which we do not feel competent. If you're clumsy on the green, how often do you play golf? If you can't see straight, how much will you enjoy billiards? Once again, sex is no exception. If you feel like a klutz in bed you are undoubtedly having sex less often than you'd really like to. Human nature being what it is, most individuals avoid facing their ineptness in bed. Many will tolerate very unsatisfying sex rather than admit ignorance or seek help, as in the following cases.

Samuel, a 26-year-old virgin, came for therapy because the last of a string of relationships had soured. Until now he had rationalized that his lack of sexual experience was the result of never having found anyone who turned him on. Then he met Beth, and they began dating seriously. Samuel thought Beth was a real knockout. She was also willing to have sex. He was interested but he didn't follow through. Finally he ran out of excuses and was forced to admit to himself his feelings of incompetence. As Samuel put it, "Up to now I thought when the right one comes along nature takes over. I guess I was fussy in dating to avoid sexual possibilities. I really don't know much about sex."

Samuel had the courage to seek help. Conventional technique therapy was all he needed. After some extensive reading and coaching, Samuel and Beth pursued their relationship on a very satisfying level. Samuel's was a rather severe case. Less serious ones are quite common among both married and single people.

Katherine and Will had been married for almost four years. Prior to their marriage they had had sex less than once a week, but attributed this to lack of opportunity. After the ceremony the pattern continued and they assumed it was the adjustment period. Finally, after four years of mediocre, biweekly sex, they decided something was wrong.

In therapy, for the first time, each expressed their doubts. Will admitted he felt inexperienced and clumsy and thus avoided sex. Katherine admitted she simply felt Will did not find her very attractive. Once again, conventional technique therapy was all that was needed.

* * *

You can tell if a poor sexual image is interfering with your sex life by looking for the following symptoms:

1. A "sour grapes" attitude or a denial of sexual interest, often expressed in one or more of the following ways:
    (a) "Sex is okay, but it isn't all it's cracked up to be!"
    (b) "What's so important about sex anyway?"
    (c) "In five minutes it's all over, so why make such a fuss?"

Such comments come from people who don't enjoy sex. Sex should be fun, and it *is* worth the time and effort to make sure you enjoy it. Anyone who thinks differently is probably uncomfortable in bed.

2. Being unusually picky about potential partners: individuals who can never find someone good enough obviously do not want to find anyone.
3. Always letting your partner take the initiative.
4. Generally feeling relieved when sex is over. These individuals feel performance anxiety during the act. After sex is over, relief comes from having made it through without a screw-up, as opposed to feeling a release of sexual tension.
5. Purposely picking the impossible or unattainable partner; that is, "I want Pauline but she's married" or "I'm

madly in love with Father Bernard" or "I only want sex with a millionaire and I haven't found one yet."

This feeling of incompetency in bed is surprisingly common. Thousands of couples suffer the ill effects of bedroom clumsiness, and generally respond well to technique therapy.

GENDER IDENTITY

We will now consider the second aspect of sexual identity: comfort with one's gender. The key question here is "Do I enjoy being a man or woman?" Many individuals are not happy with their sex. We are all familiar with the most extreme of cases, the transsexual. These individuals feel so uncomfortable with their sex they decide to have themselves surgically altered.

Here we are concerned with individuals who have moderate doubts about their sexual constitution. They may simply not feel masculine or feminine "enough," or they may feel burdened by traits which traditionally belong to the opposite sex. Examples would be a woman who enjoys being rough, bold, and aggressive, or a man who feels too sensitive and shuns competition and toughness.

These individuals may value their gender, but doubt their masculinity or femininity. Their doubts force them to seek constant confirmation of their sexual natures, most often through hypersexuality. The male may be driven to seduce as many women as often as he can. The female counterpart may wish to be seduced at every possible opportunity. (Some are content to imagine that every member of the opposite sex is "hot after their body.")

In short, these men and women use sex to quell their doubts about their sexual identity—by doing what is considered masculine or feminine, not what satisfies their sexual impulses. The pleasure they do feel comes from the act of seduction and the subsequent relief from their doubts—rather than from the ebb and flow of sexual energy and impulses.

Throughout sex they may feel conflict between what they would like to do and what is the "masculine" or "feminine" thing to do. For example, the woman may want to take the lead and set the pace, but must be coy and seductive to confirm her femininity. The man may want to be passive and pampered, but his masculine ideal requires him to be aggressive and bold. For these individuals, sex gives minimal satisfaction. No one can do the opposite of what he or she truly desires and feel sexually fulfilled. Technique-oriented sex therapy will do little for these cases.

How does one come to doubt one's sexuality? We shall consider cases which illustrate the primary causes: parental conditioning and cultural milieu.

Jack, age 29, came for therapy because his fiancée had broken off their engagement. Florence, whom he really loved, had caught him cheating. It was not his first offense. In fact, from Jack's accounts one easily got the impression that he was trying to make the sexual Hall of Fame. His sex life consisted of a series of quick seductions. He did not know much about his partners other than how good they were in bed.

As Jack spoke, it became apparent that he used the bedroom as headquarters for his campaign to prove his virility. He resisted efforts to examine the meaning of his behavior, wanting to talk only about his escapades. The therapist encouraged this by making admiring comments about his prowess. Finally, the following exchange took place.

> *Therapist.* Wow! You really showed her!
> *Jack.* Yeah! She'll never forget.
> *Therapist.* Forget what?
> *Jack.* What it's like to be laid by a real stud.
> *Therapist.* What about Jane, Marne, and the others? Do you think they got the message?
> *Jack.* Yep! They were all addicted to my cock.
> *Therapist.* You must feel really proud—like a super man, a super stud.

Jack. Yeah. Like a real hunk of masculinity.
Therapist. Tell me what it's like to feel like a real man.

Jack began to explore what he really felt beyond simply basking in the glory of his fantasy of a man. He admitted that he had always felt like a sissy. He was the youngest of three boys. His parents had wanted a girl, but gave up trying after Jack. They would occasionally put a dress on "Jackie" and ribbons in his hair—sometimes in front of company. Everyone would remark what a cut girl he'd make. This went on until about age five or six.

Around age ten Jack expressed a passing interest in his mother's crocheting. She encouraged it far beyond his natural curiosity, and he continued it to please her. One day his friends found out and teased him about being a girl. Jack swore no one would ever doubt he was a boy again. No one ever did, except Jack himself. His doubts drove his hypersexuality.

Chris came for therapy because she "could not contain herself." As she explained it, she loved to be seduced. Her problem: "I like the seduction. The sex is another matter. I think I'm too worried about disease or my reputation to enjoy it." Her list of lovers was extensive. In therapy she realized that being seduced helped reassure her that she was a very attractive woman: the more men desired her, the more feminine she felt.

Chris was also a victim of her parents' desire for an opposite-sexed child. She recalled how her father had taught her to "throw like a boy," to run faster than girls, and to arm wrestle to win. Her father, who played all kinds of sports with her, never bought any toys he deemed were for sissies and poked fun at her softer qualities: "Oh, don't you look dainty in that silly dress." Any attempt to be "feminine" was met with ridicule. Is it any wonder that she felt compelled to prove that she was attractive in a feminine way?

Both Chris and Jack were victims of deliberate behavior by

their parents to bastardize their gender. Parents may not realize their cruelty and the damaging long-term effects such behavior has on their children's sex lives when they reach adolescence and adulthood. We have been surprised at the number of clients who make similar complaints about parents. Giving bisexual names, cross-dressing toddlers, and buying unwanted, inappropriate toys are the most common offenses. As one male client put it, "I got a doll for Christmas. Can you imagine? I'm five, want a gun, a bike, or a wagon and I get a doll! I was furious and hurt, but I still got the message."

In other cases cultural milieu is responsible for creating doubts about gender. Parents rigidly enforce a cultural stereotype of masculinity or femininity. The child unwittingly tries to live up to these ideals, but never quite makes the grade. Doubts about gender inevitably surface.

This happened to Craig. His father was a rugged individual who taught his son that men don't cry ("Cut the tears, sissy!"), that men are bold and love adventure ("Get in there. Men aren't afraid of the dark"), and that men love sports and competition ("A good fight never hurt anyone!"). As Craig grew up he found at times that he *was* afraid, that he *wanted* to cry, and that he never cared one whit for bold adventures.

During adolescence he became interested in painting and music. He was a very sensitive, artistic young man; in fact, he wanted to be an artist, but became a builder out of economic necessity. Throughout his life Craig tried to supress his sensitive nature. He adopted his father's cultural stereotype but continued to have lingering doubts about his masculinity.

After fifteen years of marriage, his wife demanded that they get help for her. She wanted relief from Craig's incessant demands for more sex. She said, "Sex is fun. But too much is too much. I thought as he got older he'd let up a bit. Sometimes I think he does it because he has to."

In therapy Craig realized that his exaggerated masculine identity created a false hunger for sex. He wanted sex often and for long periods simply because he felt that's what real men do.

These cases illustrate several points about using sex to confirm sexual identity:

- It happens to men *and* women.
- Sex can never satisfy this nonsexual need. Thus, sex is never as satisfying as it should be.
- A series of seductions with several partners is not always involved. Craig, for example, never had an affair. He vented his hypersexuality in his marriage.
- Conventional technique therapy would not benefit these individuals.

Individuals who have not personalized and internalized the concept of masculine or feminine are most likely to use sex to confirm or reassure sexual identity. Each of us must decide what it means to be masculine or feminine and what constitutes a good lover. Only when we set realistic and personally meaningful standards for ourselves can we can feel "sexually" secure. When personal standards are absent, sex is mistakenly determined by an imaginary ideal or stereotype.

In summary, individuals who have doubts about their sexual prowess tend to have sex less than they'd like to. Individuals who doubt their gender tend to have sex more than they need or want to. In either case these individuals do not reap their full measure of sexual pleasure or satisfaction. Conventional technique sex therapy is best suited for the former, nonsexual sex therapy for the latter.

* * *

If you suspect that this may be happening to you or your partner:

- Examine for yourself or share your fantasies about the

ideal man/woman with your partner. List as many traits as possible, and give examples of what you mean. Then, (a) examine each trait to see how realistic and desirable it is for both you and your partner; (b) talk about how such a trait would effect each of you and your relationship.

- Pretend you are a good lover. Create a detailed fantasy about what a good lover does. Act it out with your partner. Repeat and practice. You will be surprised at how adept you can become.
- Make love while listening to music. Flow with the music, letting it dictate your moves. This will help you to realize that letting yourself go is the key ingredient to satisfying sex. Do not try to *control* your movements to please yourself or your lover. Simply give in to the feelings and impulses as they arise. This is what a good lover does. This is what leads to sexual satisfaction —following the ebb and flow of sexual feelings and impulses.

8

Sex and Self-Esteem

J.D. was arrested for solicitation. He was released on the condition that he seek therapy. In therapy, J.D. related that he would accost strangers in the men's room at a local university and offer them free sexual favors. Someone who had been frightened by his offer had called the police.

He admitted that the sexual pleasure was secondary, and that he did not really enjoy what he was doing. The thrill was in the accosting, in seeing "the stunned, questioning look . . . waiting to see if they accept or reject."

J.D.'s problem had little to do with sex. In fact, his problem was one of low self-esteem. He was using sex to confirm that, indeed, he was a worthless person. After all, "No one but a low-class piece of rubbish would do such a stupid, vulgar thing."

Fortunately, such severe problems are rare. However, everyone's sex life is affected positively or negatively by self-esteem. An individual with a good self-image (a healthy level of self-esteem) will generally pick sex partners of equal status, indulge in a variety of pleasurable acts, and satisfy his or her sexual needs. In short, sex will generally be a satisfying, pleasant experience.

On the other hand, low self-esteem has a negative influence on sexual behavior. A person with low self-esteem is more likely to pick unsavory partners, perform degrading sexual acts, sabotage his/her own pleasure, or become a performance-conscious bed partner. Sexual pleasure will be minimal. However, reduced pleasure is often the least of the concerns. More serious problems can result, as in J.D.'s case.

J.D. had many nonsexual motives and feelings which needed to be separated from sex and resolved. First, he had to admit to himself that the sexual pleasure he gained from his behavior was minimal. We accomplished this by having him go through each part of his interactions in the men's room mentally, focusing on the accompanying feelings. J.D. learned that he felt:

(a) strong and in control when his "victim" looked shocked or afraid;

(b) grateful and pleased when someone gave him a warm reception;

(c) humiliated and submissive when he got on his knees to do his thing;

(d) accomplished and excited when his victim became erect;

(e) sexually excited as he performed the act;

(f) relieved when it was completed;

(g) terrible a few minutes afterward; and

(h) driven to do it all over again to avoid facing the guilt and negative feelings it brought out.

Each feeling had to be understood and worked through to some resolution. Take (a), for example. J.D. felt strong because someone was afraid of him; he felt in charge because he could decide whether or not to follow through with the act. These feelings related to the rest of his life. J.D. confessed that he had grown up feeling like the proverbial 98-pound weakling, the runt of the litter. His father was an authoritarian bully who had kept J.D. under his thumb all through childhood. As an adult J.D. was very passive and often let others take advantage of him. He was surprised to learn of the connection between these experiences and his sexual behavior.

J.D. also reported feeling grateful and pleased when his victims agreed, interpreting their acquiescence to the act as acceptance of him as a person. Hence the feelings of gratitude and pleasure. In effect, J.D. thought so little of himself that he was willing to be humiliated in return—for one brief moment—for the feeling that someone liked him.

As therapy continued it became obvious that all of this behavior was tied to low self-esteem. Therapy consisted of resolving all of these feelings, building his self-esteem, and training him in assertiveness. We later included technique-oriented sex therapy to help him feel confident of being able to establish a wholesome sexual relationship.

Self-esteem problems this serious are rare. However, low self-esteem does influence many thousands of sex lives to a lesser degree. The following patterns show a few of the more common ways this happens.

Choosing Unsavory Partners

Individuals in this category can never seem to find respectable partners. They reinforce a poor self-image by becoming sexually involved with unsavory people.

This happened to Tom. He was single, attractive, had a Ph.D. in physics, yet seemed unable to find any appropriate partners. He felt that educated women were boring and not interested in sex and fun. Women who attracted him usually turned out to be less educated, less responsible, and less morally principled than he. His latest affair was with a woman of doubtful character whose two lovers decided that one more was too many and worked Tom over to make their point. That's when he came for therapy.

Tom capsulized the nonsexual dynamics behind his behavior during his first session. "When I came to in a dark alley, reeking of blood and booze like a common drunk . . . I never felt so humiliated, so worthless. . . . I suddenly realized this is what I've been doing to myself all along, getting involved with the wrong kind of people. That's when I knew I needed help."

Tom's problem was his low self-esteem. His parents pushed him to achieve beyond his own desires. He had wanted to be a marine biologist and work on an oceanic research ship. His father, an Air Force major, demanded more of his son. His mother, a socialite of considerable renown, wanted a son she could brag about to her admirers.

In therapy Tom learned to accept and satisfy his own needs, desires, and ambitions instead of living up to the expectations of his parents.

Unsavory (Perverted) Sex

Unsavory sex includes any sexually unconventional acts which the indulgee associates with wierd, strange, or sick (perverted) individuals. In other words, anything a person considers perverted *is* perverted for him or her. When individuals become involved in such acts they are using sex to confirm low self-esteem. Often they are well aware of this.

For example, Peter, age 32, came for therapy because he enjoyed the humiliation he felt when his wife whipped him. He felt degraded, but couldn't stop the behavior. His wife did not want to continue and suggested therapy.

Sean, age 28, came for therapy after his wife learned that he had had fellatio with several men and threatened to leave. Sean admitted that he felt humiliated and degraded, rather than aroused, during the act; yet he continued the behavior until his wife found out.

Neither of these men had a sexual problem. Their problems centered around a poor self-image. Treatment is two-pronged. First, the therapist must help the individual become aware of the long-term effects of the behavior, that is, the feeling of worthlessness. This feeling must be separated from whatever pleasure the sex act may have. Second, the client must be taught to see him or herself as a good, worthy person. The therapist can teach the client to focus on and appreciate personal strengths.

".... AND THAT'S ALL I WANT HER TO TRY. THAT'S NOT SO WEIRD IS IT DOCTOR? DOCTOR?! DOCTOR SAY SOMETHING !"

Promiscuity

When we know that others accept, admire, or respect us, it's easier to respect and value ourselves. Some individuals use sex to gain acceptance and admiration. By giving sex they hope to feel important, needed, and special: they use sex to build self-esteem. Unfortunately, any good feelings from such transactions are short-lived. In fact, the usual long-term effect is depression.

Mary Lou, age 22, came for therapy after feeling depressed for several months. She did not understand her depression because she was having a "super fantastic" social life. Her weekends were filled. She was extremely popular with men and always had a party to attend.

Mary Lou described herself as a liberated woman who led a very active sex life. It was not unusual for her to end up in bed on the first date. She did not feel any guilt and often was the one to initiate sex. But in therapy Mary Lou realized that she valued the feeling of being "in demand" more than she did the act of sex itself. She came to understand that she was using sex to gain self-esteem, to feel important and needed.

Sabotaging Your Own Pleasure

Individuals with low self-esteem often undermine their own pleasure. We typically find one of the following patterns in a couple's sex life when one or both of the partners experience low self-esteem.

1. Couples can place too many stipulations on having a good time, often because of feelings of guilt. (The chapter on guilt is appropriate for these cases.) Basically these couples place a low priority on sex, putting it next in line after the kids, the lawn, the housework, the office work, and TV.

There are zillions of excuses for not having fun, but not one good reason. If you really enjoy sex but find yourself making excuses, ask yourself, "Do I deserve to have a good time or don't I?" Your self-esteem will tell.

2. Individuals can also sabotage their pleasure after the fact. Once they've had sex, they review the experience and begin to find fault: "Well, the climax was good, but too short!" "Foreplay was great, but I wish I would have had more visual stimulation." "It was really good, but I tried to hold back too long."

This type of individual has a pretty good time, but then proceeds to ruin it with a critical analysis.

This second pattern happened to Peter and Alice. They often had fantastic sex. Just as often, Peter would give a critical, play-by-play analysis of the act. At first, Alice thought it was cute and that Peter was out to have even better sex next time. "Next time" never came. The analysis was always negative. Sex, for Peter, became a search for perfection. He came to believe he had a sexual problem because sex was never perfect. Alice felt bad for Peter and for herself. She thought his disappointment might be her fault. That's when she insisted on therapy.

Good sex has occurred any time you are left feeling happy and satisfied. Any search for *perfect* sex will sabotage your own pleasure. It usually indicates a problem with self-esteem and/or guilt.

3. Couples can also sabotage their fun by *not* planning their good time, by having sex just when mother normally calls, just when the kids come home, or just before they have to rush to an appointment or catch a bus. Curiously, when you ask these couples why they don't plan sex at more convenient times their standard reply is, "What? And lose spontaneity? We want it to be natural!" But there is nothing natural about an interrupting telephone call; nor is there anything unnatural about locking the bedroom door to keep the kids out.

Aiming to Please

Probably the most common bedroom symptom of low self-esteem is always pleasing your partner at your own expense. Pleasing a partner can be and is a source of added pleasure. But your partner's pleasure must be sought in addition to—not instead of—your own.

If the "aim to please" precludes or ignores personal enjoyment, true sexual satisfaction and pleasure are minimal. Most of the satisfaction that "pleasers" experience comes from a job well done, not from sexual release. These individuals become very performance-oriented. Their pleasure and satisfaction is determined by the extent and degree of their partner's enjoyment. In other words, the pleaser is using sex to build self-esteem, to obtain admiration, to feel important, competent, and needed.

SELF-ESTEEM AND GUILT

Self-esteem and guilt are closely related: individuals with low self-esteem are often subject to considerable guilt. Thus the same sexual behavior may be motivated by either or both. One person may have sex with unsavory partners primarily because he or she doesn't feel worthy of a better partner. Another individual may behave the same way—primarily because of guilt ("I'm doing something evil; therefore I must be punished with the risk of disease, etc."). Likewise, a couple may sabotage their pleasure out of guilt for having done something wrong or because they feel they do not deserve to have a good time.

How can we determine which motive is the primary force? Consider the case of a guilt-ridden individual. He or she is saying, "I'm bad because I'm doing something bad, wrong, evil." In early childhood this person received negative messages about sex while the messages about personal competency, adequacy, and worth were neutral or positive. Treatment consists of examining and restructuring the individual's acquired attitudes and beliefs about sex.

The situation is different when sex is driven by low self-esteem. Here the individual is saying, "I don't deserve to have fun or enjoy myself." In early childhood he or she received negative messages about personal competency, adequacy, or worth, while sex was presented in a neutral or positive light. Treatment would center around examining the self-image and building self-esteem.

Of course, individuals may have received negative messages in both areas. Cases where low self-esteem and guilt interact are more complicated and will be discussed in the next chapter. Exposing and examining these internalized messages, past and present, will help individuals and couples understand the patterns of their sex lives. For a more detailed discussion of multiple motives, consult Appendix I.

Individuals who did not learn as children to feel worthy and good must continue to earn self-esteem as adults. As youngsters they learned to gain self-esteem by pleasing others. This pattern continues in their adult life. The bedroom serves as one more place where they can make themselves feel better or confirm their self-esteem. The cycle can be broken only by establishing a positive self-image independent of sex.

* * *

Individuals who have been taught that sex is "dirty" or sinful should try the suggestions in the chapter on guilt. Individuals who suffer from low self-esteem must learn what they like, want, and need. Above all they must learn to feel that they deserve pleasure and satisfaction. Learning all this after years of pleasing others may be difficult. Some of the following activities may help.

Learning Likes and Needs

- Take turns; have one partner be completely passive while the other is active. No matter how great the temptation, the passive partner must not do anything but lie there, enjoying and communicating with words, moans, groans, smiles, and so on, how pleasurable each action is. Get into the good feeling of having someone please you. Focus strictly on the pleasure you feel. If concern for your partner begins to disturb your enjoyment, simply remind yourself that "Now it's my turn. He/she will be next." Switch roles.
- Discuss with your partner how difficult or easy each

role was. Give plenty of positive feedback on the things you did enjoy. This will encourage future re-engagements.

- Alternate playing king and queen for a night. One night the queen must decide who does what to whom; the next night the king decides. This will help you learn to be assertive and to take responsibility for what you like and want.
- Consult the suggestions at the end of the chapter on atonement.

Developing Self-Appreciation

- Argue with yourself about your right to enjoy and to be pleasured. Every time doubt sets in remind yourself of the many things you do for your partner. Don't be bashful: count everything. They add up and each one is important.
- List all your good qualities (in and out of the bedroom). Enjoy and lavishly praise yourself for each one. Remind yourself that you are unique, that there is no one else like you.
- List the ways each of these qualities makes your life more enjoyable and the ways each one brings added joy to those you love. Remind yourself that you are unique and that only you can have this effect on others.
- Have your partner draw up a list of your good qualities and the ways that these qualities make life easier, more pleasant, and more satisfying for him/her.
- Reread these lists as often as you can. Let the different items sink in and relish each one.
- Learn to accept who you are. Stop expecting perfection.

9

Sex and Guilt

Guilt is that gnawing, uncomfortable feeling you get when you've done something you shouldn't have. Anyone can feel guilty about anything—and everything. Sex is no exception. Nothing can ruin a good time in bed as quickly or as completely as guilt. But where does sexual guilt originate?

Cultural beliefs and parental attitudes shape our feelings about sex. From day one we are given contradictory messages about what is right or wrong: "There's nothing shameful about our bodies, but don't look, touch, or enjoy." "Sex is wonderful and beautiful, but it's not right unless you're married. Once married it becomes your sacred duty." With all these contradictions, no one can totally escape feeling some form of sexual guilt. Thus it's important to understand how guilt influences sexual behavior.

We are concerned here with two types of guilt: guilt over *not* having sex, and guilt over having sex. Single persons and married couples can be victims of the latter. The former only effects couples committed or married to each other. Both are surprisingly common. Both lessen sexual pleasure. We shall begin with guilt over not having sex.

GUILT OVER NOT INDULGING

No one should feel guilt for not having sex, but many people do—for two reasons. First, we are taught that it is our duty as married people to have sex with our mates. When we don't, we feel we are neglecting our marital responsibility. Second, many of us feel responsible for our partner's sexual satisfaction. If we don't have sex as often as he or she wants it, we feel inadequate. If we want it more often than our partner we feel greedy, like we're asking for too much. Either way, guilt moves in.

Almost everyone occasionally experiences these feelings. Intermittent bouts with this type of guilt are annoying but the effect on sexual pleasure is temporary. Sex just isn't as enjoyable when it is done out of a sense of duty. The solution to this problem is to discuss these feelings with your mate.

When there is a serious discrepancy between a couple's sexual desires, guilt has a profound effect. The less active partner feels sexually inadequate, and will respond in one of two ways. The first is to become preoccupied with feelings of sexual inadequacy and to avoid sex as much as possible. When sex does occur it is laden with anxiety. The less active partner focuses solely on performance and the other partner's satisfaction; that is, "Am I good enough to satisfy my partner?" or "I hope this is a really good one so he/she will be satisfied for a while." Under such conditions, sexual pleasure is at a minimum. Interest in sex will decrease and the feelings of sexual inadequacy will increase.

The more active partner will usually begin to feel oversexed and unfulfilled, and may seek satisfaction elsewhere or demand more sex at home. Eventually the active partner feels guilty for wandering or for demanding too much.

The second course of action is to increase sexual activity to please the more active partner. The less active partner agrees to sex even though the mood or interest isn't there. Again, sex becomes a chore instead of a delight. No one can continually indulge in sex only to please someone else. Jealousy and resentment will surface. It's only human to feel jealous of the partner who enjoys sex more all the time. Eventually the less active partner will feel used and will resent servicing the other.

Resolving Guilt Over Not Having Sex

Occassional feelings of guilt or inadequacy are best dealt with immediately and directly. Discuss the situation with your partner. A supportive, understanding comment will usually do the trick; for example, "I'm not really on fire with passion, but I'll be glad to satisfy you." It's easier to help your partner find some satisfaction in an understanding atmosphere.

Many couples report that what started off as sex "just to please" turned into an exciting, satisfying experience. This seems to occur only when couples encourage each other. The horny partner must be willing to make a little more than the usual effort to arouse the other. The unaroused partner in turn must show appreciation for these efforts. In such a supportive atmosphere it's easier to ignite the spark of mutual passion. It helps if you see your mate's arousal as a compliment to your sexiness.

For more serious discrepancies between partners' sex drives, the following may be helpful:

- Keep in mind that sexual satisfaction is each partner's own responsibility. It becomes a mutual problem because one partner's satisfaction and pleasure affects the other's.
- Together, look for ways to make sex more satisfying for both partners. As sex becomes more enjoyable for the less active partner, interest and enthusiasm will increase. Anyone having sex that is both pleasurable and satisfying will feel sexually adequate and will desire sex more often. It is a fact of human nature that we want to do the things we enjoy and do competently as often as possible.

- The less active partner may simply not know what is pleasing to him/herself. Experiment.
- The more active partner may feel he/she is not getting enough simply because the other partner responds with little enthusiasm. This may be exactly what creates the discrepancy in the first place. It is important to discuss these feelings openly and honestly.

GUILT OVER HAVING SEX

We tend to associate guilt over having sex with unmarried people. However, it is also surprisingly common among the married. In our culture most of us have been conditioned to feel that sex before marriage is wrong, dirty, immoral. We assume that when people marry they will automatically enjoy guiltless sex. This is not the case.

We adopt these voices from the past as our own. What was imposed on us earlier by others becomes internalized and replaced by self-imposed restrictions on sexual pleasure. Thus, when couples begin having sex, married or not, guilt is there. For most couples, fortunately, it is not severe. Nonetheless it exists and lessens sexual pleasure.

More serious problems arise when guilt is severe and the guilt-ridden individual has strong dependency needs. These individuals do not have sex as often as they'd like, and when they do have sex they don't enjoy it. Typically, therapists refer to them as "morally inhibited" and prescribe the following type of therapy.

The couple is told to completely refrain from sex. The therapist then grants them progressive permissions: to hold hands, then to kiss, neck, pet, and finally to have intercourse. This approach is based on the assumption that the couple should habituate to sex in small steps so that their conscience will not rebel against the "authority of the doctor."

In many cases, this works. However, we believe that this

approach only perpetuates a maladaptive pattern. The motives influencing the sexual behavior are actually nonsexual. These couples earn self-esteem by giving up sex to preserve or increase self-worth or to please others. They are thinking, "If I don't have sex, mom, dad, or some deity will think I'm wonderful." Or "If I don't indulge as often as everyone else I'm a more disciplined person."

Dependency, fostered by low self-esteem, is the critical problem here. These individuals absorb and accept whatever is presented to them. They don't analyze, scrutinize, and make their own judgments. In short, they rely on others to make their decisions, establish their attitudes, and grant them permission. The therapy technique described above perpetuates this pattern. Instead, therapy should help the couple examine their underlying lack of self-esteem and their dependency as well as their attitudes toward sex.

In sum, "morally inhibited" individuals refrain from having sex to earn self-esteem or the approval of others, whether human or divine. They fear that, in having sex, they will lose this approval and consequently, their self-esteem. It is this fear that prevents sexual enjoyment. Technique therapy does work, in that these couples can learn to enjoy sex to some degree. However, nonsexual therapy will bring about sweeping changes in the couple's relationship and in their overall adjustment. The following case illustrates this point.

Mr. O. was 53 years old when he was admitted to the hospital. He had a history of depression since late adolescence. Sex wasn't important to him because he never enjoyed it when he had it. According to his wife, they had not had sex for over 20 years. Mrs. O. didn't share his attitude and in the last 10 years had taken him through a series of doctors and tests. At one marriage clinic they were told, "It's been so long since he had sex, and considering his age, it's unlikely anything can be done." At this point Mr. O. began running red lights and suffering from crying spells. His wife had him hospitalized out of desperation.

After his depression subsided we began working on Mr. O's sex problem. We concluded that he had always depended on parental approval and permission for everything, including having sex. Instead of a technique approach, we decided to resurrect his deceased father. Mr. O. had to argue with his father about anything and everything, and they eventually came around to sex. At one point Mr. O. shouted, "I'm god-damned tired of listening to you and doing what you say. Just 'cause you hated women and sex and God knows what else. . . . The fact is you hated everything and everybody. . . . I'm going to have sex if I want to!"

This was Mr. O.'s turning point. He started going home for weekend visits. A few weeks later, Mrs. O. reported, "He's a changed man. He came home with some flowers. He smiles and, ah, . . . well, we don't have that problem anymore."

We followed the O.'s for six months. Their entire life changed. Mr. O. quit his job and started a new career at twice his old salary. He went from an apathetic, dependent, passive old man to a vibrant, independent human being who discovered his sexuality at 53.

We gave no sexual instructions other than "Do what you feel up to." The rest was Mr. O.'s responsibility. He had to break his dependency patterns, and to start making his *own* decisions about everything, including sex. A technique therapist might have corrected the sex problem, although even that is doubtful. It was at a sex clinic that he'd heard, "It doesn't look promising."

Mr. O.'s was a very serious case. However, he demonstrated how even "hopeless" cases can be helped. His case also demonstrates the value of looking beyond the "sex problem." While guilt may not be as severe in most cases, it is present nonetheless, taking its toll on pleasure.

Repetition Compulsion

Severe guilt also can create a compulsion to have more sex. We call this a "repetition compulsion," so named by Theodore

Reich. Basically, it consists of repeating the act that produces severe guilt in an effort to squelch the guilt. In other words, you try to convince yourself that the act is acceptable by doing it repeatedly.

This is how it works. You have sex. You experience immediate pleasure. Later the guilt begins to surface. You repeat the same act to recapture the good feelings and avoid facing the guilt. Each time the guilt resurfaces, you repeat the act to squelch the guilt. You want to avoid realizing that you have done something that is against your moral upbringing, so you keep yourself focused on the immediate pleasure. It's like trying to convince yourself that something that feels so good cannot possibly be wrong.

Repetition compulsions have three characteristics. First, the desire and demand for sex increases. The individual wants to have sex longer and more often. Second, in spite of the increased duration and frequency, sexual satisfaction is minimal. The individual cannot seem to get enough. Third, the afflicted individual is unaware that it is guilt that motivates the sex. He or she may have a vague awareness that something is missing, but generally feels that sex is great and cannot wait for the next time. Indeed, these individuals are always focused on the next time, which helps prevent the guilt from surfacing. As long as the guilt is not faced and resolved, the repetition compulsion continues to dominate sex.

* * *

The most common victims of "repetition compulsion" are individuals who:

- fail to think beyond the immediate consequences of their behavior.
- accept the doctrine of others without giving thought to their own moral or spiritual values.
- were likely to have had strict moral values imposed on

them by their parents. The guilt that results from not meeting these exceptionally high moral standards causes the compulsion.

This type of guilt over having sex is a little complicated. It can be resolved only by replacing the early sexual proscriptions and parental dictates with more sensible, realistic values. Here are some things you can try.

- Think about sex: what kinds of negative messages did you hear from your parents? Examine them and decide if they are realistic. Then (a) argue with these voices from the past, countering each negative attitude with a positive one; and (b) repeat until you feel that you have conquered this negative intrusion into your bedroom.
- On the left side of a sheet of paper, list all the negative thoughts you have about sex: On the right side, counter each negative thought with several positive ones. Do this until you cannot come up with any more negatives.
- Play devil's advocate. Have the more inhibited partner bring up a negative attitude about sex. The other partner should argue and demonstrate the irrationality of the belief. Then reverse roles. Be convincing—convert your partner.
- Fantasize about sex. Think of things you'd secretly like to do, but feel too shy to bring up. Remind yourself that you and your partner have every right to enjoy them. Be emphatic! If negative thoughts intrude, counter each one with an assertion that sex is good and healthy. Demand your natural right to pleasure.
- Think of negative proscriptions against sex. Now push them to the extreme: say, "Sex is dirty"; "Only slobs do it"; "You should be ashamed to even think of the act"; "Your hand should fall off for touching yourself"; "You deserve to be punished"; "You deserve hell." As

you go on, the ridiculousness of your negative attitude will become apparent.

It is obvious that guilt can enter our sex lives on several levels. In fact, very few individuals in our society reach adulthood without experiencing some sexual guilt. Ridding ourselves of this unwarranted feeling requires considerable thought and effort. We must examine the messages we received in our early years and the ones we presently receive from society. We must evaluate them objectively, determine which are appropriate, and discard the ones that interfere with our sexual pleasure. Only then can we enjoy sex without guilt.

10

Sex to Mask Anger

Most of the time sex is used to give and receive enjoyment. However, it can also be used to give pain, to degrade, to humiliate, and to punish. In this chapter we shall discuss the various ways sex is used as an outlet for some of these aggressive impulses.

MASKING GENERAL ANGER

Anger is a difficult emotion to express. We can't always vent our anger when we initially feel it. And we can't always direct it at the person who caused it, for example, the parent, boss, or dear friend we don't want to offend. But these negative feelings do not disappear. Repressed anger always seeks expression, often surfacing at inappropriate times and directed at the wrong person. For example, the boss yells at you. You come home and yell at your mate, who yells at the child, who kicks the dog, who tears up the newspaper. This is a common phenomenon that most of us learn to tolerate.

Some people resist expressing anger in any form because they were taught that such expression is wrong. They simply repress it. The repressed anger builds up until it becomes difficult to control. Such people are irritable and abrupt in their interactions, although never quite openly angry. They seem unable to control their abruptness. Indeed, they cannot. Their unexpressed anger seeks any outlet for irritability and abruptness; the bedroom is not exempt. In fact, some types of sexual activity are ideal stimuli for triggering the repressed anger (biting, squeezing, and so on—see the table on p. 158).

Individuals who use sex as an outlet for repressed anger are likely to be seen as rough, wild, or excessively passionate lovers. Frequently they pump maddeningly and demand long periods of harsh, active intercourse. Complaints about their excesses are usually met with defenisve replies: "You're just too delicate!"; "I can't help it. I get carried away. Don't you?"

Often their victim-partners will accept the blame and learn

" I'M NOT SURE IF YOU JUST MADE LOVE
TO ME OR RAN ME OVER WITH A STEAM ROLLER !! "

to tolerate the roughness. This is unfortunate because in doing so they forfeit their own sexual pleasure. It is difficult to enjoy sex when being mistreated. Furthermore, allowing a partner to be excessive in this way only perpetuates the pattern of using sex to release pent-up anger.

How can you tell whether your partner is releasing pent-up anger? If, after sex, you feel that you've been bullied or mistreated, chances are good that your lover was carried away by the passion of anger, not of sex or love.

What can the angry lover do? The following activities might help:

- Write the words "I am pissed off because. . . . " Complete the sentence with whatever comes to mind. Repeat this activity every time that undirected feeling of anger surfaces. Once an item is written down you can do one of two things: (a) Expand on it. Describe how the anger feels, going into as much detail as possible. (b) Punch a pillow as you shout out your beef. The louder and angrier, the better. Try yelling "I'm pissed off because . . . and I'm not going to take it any more!"
- Sit in a quiet room. Pretend there is a trunk at the other end that is full of your anger. The things you are angry about all have their own personalities. Bring them out one at a time. Introduce yourself. Get to know each other. Carry on a conversation about the what, when, how, and why of your feelings. Make friends, but let your anger know that from now on you are in charge, that you will recognize it, accept it, and let it have its due, but in a constructive, nonsexual way.
- Consult a therapist. You probably don't enjoy life in general and may miss much of the pleasure of being alive.

ANGER TOWARD YOUR PARTNER

In any relationship one partner inevitably does things which provoke the other partner's anger or annoyance. What happens to this anger is of paramount importance. Left unexpressed, it smolders and can seriously hamper sexual pleasure.

There are four basic ways that negative emotions can seep into the bedroom.

Withholding Sex

Sex can be withheld out of anger. This is understandable: it is difficult to want to give pleasure to a person with whom you are angry. In such cases it's best to discuss the problem and resolve the anger. Then you can decide if you want sex, and anger will not interfere with your pleasure.

However, individuals are sometimes unaware of the connection between anger and withholding sex. Repressed anger has a way of surfacing as a numbing headache, a low back pain, or an anti-romantic mood. People who internalize anger are most apt to fall into this category. Often they feel a certain smugness, that withholding sex is justified. They may even feel grateful for the psychosomatic excuse. Their attitude can be verbalized as "My headache serves you right."

This tactic is really self-defeating. Angry individuals suffer twice, once for the earlier hurt and again by depriving themselves of sexual pleasure. A repeated pattern of withholding sex is a symptom of a more serious problem.

Making Inconsiderate Demands

Inconsiderate demands also mask angry feelings. They may take the form of unconventional sex or positions that the victim-partner finds repulsive. If you want something that your partner finds distasteful, discussion and gradual initiation are warranted. It is one thing to ask, another to demand. The key difference is in taking your partner's feelings into consideration.

Other common forms of inconsideration stemming from anger include penetrating before lubrication, demanding entrance before your partner is fully erect, racing through the act, leaving your partner hanging, using excessive roughness,

pumping dry, and making negative comments about your partner's prowess.

We all may enter too soon, rush through the act, or get too
rough on occasion. This is no cause for concern. It is a pattern
of repeated inconsideration which is a symptom of unresolved
anger.

Loss of Interest

Sometimes anger makes one partner lead the other on and
then withdraw. Phil and Zeta came for counseling for this very
reason. Zeta would always initiate sex when completing the
act was bound to be impossible. In the morning she would
behave seductively when she and Phil had to rush off to work.
On nights when Phil had to do paperwork at home, she wore
her sexiest nighties. Yet, when there was ample time, Zeta
would show no interest, and curl up with a book instead. Both
she and Phil were at a loss to explain her behavior. They felt
that sex was good when they had it.

It turned out that Zeta was very angry that Phil expected
her to work and keep house as well. She did not feel justified
in being angry, because Phil did have to put more hours into
his work, but she was angry just the same. After Zeta explained
her position, she and Phil resolved to get a part-time house-
keeper. This worked out well and their sex life returned to
normal.

Impotence and Frigidity

Many therapists believe that anger and resentment can
cause these well-known sexual malfunctions. We too have
found that repressed anger or resentment is usually the force
behind impotence or frigidity. When you are angry it is difficult
to enjoy sex and even more difficult to help your partner enjoy
it. Becoming impotent or frigid is a way to vent your anger by
depriving your partner of pleasure or satisfaction while avoiding responsibility for your angry feelings.

Initially, impotence or frigidity is met with support and understanding from the nonaffected partner. The irony lies in the long-term effect. The nonaffected partner eventually becomes impatient and angry with the impotent/frigid partner. The battle focuses on who didn't do what sexually and whose fault it is. The real, nonsexual anger is lost. Once again sex becomes the center of a nonsexual problem.

Occasionally the source of resentment or anger seems trivial, ludicrous, or immature, as in Joanne's case. She had had a good sex life prior to marriage, but shortly afterward, could no longer reach orgasm. She and her husband claimed sex was enjoyable, and neither partner's sexual history revealed any clues about the cause of their problem. But we could hear and feel the resentment as Joanne spoke about her husband, even though it was never anchored to anything specific.

Joanne finally discovered the source of her resentment. Prior to marriage she had been the center of attention—the life of singles parties—and had dated several prominent men. Marriage ended the social whirl. She blamed Bill for the loss of attention and the decrease in her sense of importance. When she resolved these feelings, their sex life returned to normal.

* * *

Individuals who are most likely to allow anger to infiltrate their bedroom are those who are unable to express anger when appropriate, who always defer to others, who are afraid to ask for what they want, who believe good people never get angry. All people get angry. It is important to resolve the anger. No one can enjoy sex with anger lurking at the bedroom door.

The best way to prevent anger from influencing your sex life is to deal with negative feelings as they arise. Sometimes it is impossible to do so immediately. But it is important to discuss and resolve the issue as soon as possible. Anger and resentment do not just go away. Inevitably they will resurface and cause problems.

If you suspect anger is the hidden partner in your bedroom, here are some things you can try:

- Make a list of all your partner's faults. Think about each one and how angry it makes you. Fantasize what you'd like to say and do about it. Polish up the words, confront your partner, and discuss the problem. Emphasize *your* feelings and look for solutions together.
- Have a bitch session, each partner taking two minutes to say anything without being interrupted. No name-calling. Stick to facts. Then pick one bitch that both partners feel is important and discuss that one to resolution.
- Have a pillow fight. Let everything out. Verbalize as you go: "That's for the time your damned cigar burned the rug!" "That's for burning the dinner!"
- Lock yourself in a room. *Not the bedroom*, however—you don't want to condition yourself to express anger there. As loudly as you can, call out all your pet peeves about your marriage. The best time to do this is when no one else is around.
- Try the suggestions at the end of the next chapter.

You may also be letting anger influence your sex life by having revenge affairs or withholding sexual favorites from your partner. These tactics often backfire, creating many new problems—as we shall see in the next chapter.

11

Sex for Revenge

Mrs. G. was in a panic. She had been shopping at a local department store when she felt an irresistible urge to have sex with the clerk, a total stranger. Her only escape was to leave the store in the middle of a purchase. Mrs. G. had been through this before, but she was particularly concerned because she had been married only one year when it all began.

Mrs. G. came to therapy totally disillusioned by her marriage. After the ceremony her husband had changed completely. He became unaffectionate and emotionally cruel, often abusing her with snide humor or practical jokes. Mrs. G. received little sympathy or support from her family or friends, who merely told her that nobody is perfect.

She felt trapped, helpless, and very angry. Any attempt to reason with her husband met with more abuse. Mrs. G. could not bring herself to end a new marriage. She was even tormented by thoughts that the problem was her fault or that she deserved such treatment, feelings that these recent sexual urges seemed to confirm.

In therapy Mrs. G. finally realized that she felt these "urges" because she was angry with her husband and wanted to hurt him. She was unable to get through to him verbally or emotionally. Her husband was the jealous type. By having sex with another man she would completely devastate him.

If Mrs. G. had given in to her urges, she would have used sex to seek revenge against her husband. We doubt that it would have been very enjoyable or satisfying. Using sex to get revenge seldom is. In most cases it backfires or creates further problems. Yet many people use sex to get even with their partners. We shall consider two basic patterns of revenge: active and passive.

ACTIVE REVENGE

Active revenge involves taking direct action in retaliation for a past hurt. Revenge affairs are one way the injured party may satisfy the need to even the score, but they are seldom sexually pleasurable or satisfying.

Partners seeking revenge are usually in a hurry and full of anger. Their choice of new partners may leave much to be desired. It is not uncommon to be used or abused in such hasty affairs, which only compounds the hurt. Even when such an affair goes well, guilt eventually creeps in and self-esteem plummets. In the end, the partners who seek revenge become angry with themselves *and* their mates, leaving no one to turn to for support and understanding.

Revenge affairs are inadvisable for several reasons. First, the partner who has the initial affair never accepts the avenger's affair, arguing that "Just because I fooled around doesn't mean it was right." Second, it is always more difficult to work through a double hurt than a single indiscretion. Third, most couples regret these affairs; they end up feeling cheap and immature.

This happened to Millie and Lawrence. Lawrence had a one-nighter with a stranger he met while on a business trip. This

was not typical of Lawrence, who valued fidelity and held traditional values and beliefs. In the midst of intolerable guilt, he
confessed his indiscretion, begged forgiveness, and swore it
would never happen again. Millie was devastated.

Their sex life ended abruptly. Millie felt she could not have
sex with someone she couldn't trust. "In fact," she later reported, "I thoroughly despised and hated him. I couldn't understand how he could do this. We had often discussed how
important the old values were in our marriage. And don't think
I didn't have opportunities," she continued. "I was tempted in
the past but I gave up the idea because I loved Lawrence."

Millie could not resolve her anger and hurt and at the next
opportunity had an affair. Lawrence did not understand her
"what's good for the goose is good for the gander" philosophy.
He was fit to be tied: "After I humiliated myself, begged for
pardon, made a clean slate, and gave my solemn oath, she went
and did this! With a local big-mouth. It's all over town!" he
lamented.

Millie and Lawrence had a series of revenge affairs. As Millie
explained, "for a while we were having sex with everyone but
each other. When our arguments became physical we decided
to break up. A friend recommended we try therapy before
throwing in the towel."

In this case the revenge affair was clearly more costly than
the initial hurt. Not only did Millie and Lawrence lose trust
in each other, they both lost self-respect. Lawrence summed it
up: "I can't believe two civilized people, who supposedly love
each other, can behave worse than wild animals. I didn't think
either one of us could stoop this low." Revenge affairs almost
never work. They only confuse the issue and create new problems.

An injured party may also seek revenge in the bedroom during sex, often with neither party being aware that revenge is
the motive. This happened to Fred and Frances. According to
Frances, Fred was ruining sex for her. He did this in one of

two ways: either he would bite her nipples too hard, or he would pull out, after pumping for a while, and want to have oral sex. In both cases, Frances would turn cold. "Fred would get his and I'd get frustrated," she complained. Fred was well aware that Frances did not like either act, but claimed that he would get carried away or forget. This had been going on for about six months when Frances finally refused to have sex any longer.

When they finally explored the problem, Fred admitted that he was oversensitive about the size of his penis. Frances felt that he was adequate, but recently, in jest, she had given his penis the pet name "Tiny Tim." Fred claimed he did not mind, but her joking about it to others was more than he could tolerate. Apparently, Frances had revealed the nickname at a party. Everyone was joking about going home to bed and she had said something about "taking care of Tiny Tim." Everyone had laughed—including Fred, who seemed to take it in stride. Their sex problems peaked soon after.

Fred was deeply hurt that Frances had made such a comment in public. He also realized that he did not really like the name "Tiny Tim." He designed his bedroom behavior to get even with Frances, ruining her fun in retaliation for insulting his masculine pride. In the process he deprived himself of his own pleasure. Frances agreed to drop the nickname and their problems subsided.

PASSIVE REVENGE

Passive revenge, which is surprisingly common, involves withholding something from your partner in retaliation for some minor indiscretion or fault. This tactic is relatively mild, one partner simply refusing to do the other's sexual favorites. Essentially, this partner is pouting: "You hurt my feelings, so I won't let you be on top tonight"; or "I'm not in the mood for that, after you yelled at me and criticized my cooking." If the punishing partner openly states what is wrong, the couple is free to work it out or drop it. If the matter is not discussed, the "offending" partner may never even know that he or she is being punished.

This is exactly what happened between Rob and Liz. Rob had certain unexpressed expectations: he wanted his house neat, his meals prepared, and so on; Liz was supposed to greet him enthusiastically and be affectionate and understanding on command. If she did not perform any of her duties adequately, he deprived her of her bedroom favorites. Yet Liz never seemed to learn. Rob became perplexed, and he began to think she was just plain stubborn and a slob to boot.

One day, in an angry, critical mood, Rob screamed, "Don't you want better sex? Even a monkey would have learned by now!" Liz was dumbfounded and demanded an explanation. Rob described his system of rewards and punishments—how he refused to do what he knew Liz liked if she failed as a housewife. Liz exclaimed, in utter disbelief, "So that's the problem! And all the time I thought you were a lousy lover."

This case beautifully illustrates the irony of revenge. It backfires! Avengers really punish themselves.

* * *

People who cannot deal with hurt feelings and cannot express anger directly and openly are most likely to use sex for revenge. When they are hurt they tend to internalize their anger and pout, rather than reveal and discuss their feelings. The anger held inside may suddenly burst out in a revenge affair or some other act designed to hurt. Those who choose revenge place total blame for their anger and hurt on their partners, which prevents the couple from resolving any of the underlying issues.

Those who have problems expressing hurt and anger directly can try these strategies:

- Next time your partner hurts you and you cannot express or discuss it, try this: pretend that you are the anger you have just swallowed. Think of the ways you are going to get out and get even with your mate. Be specific; don't hold back. And don't be embarassed by the violence of your desires—everyone has them. When you see the full effect of your anger, it will be easier to discuss with your partner.

- Make a list of your partner's traits and habits that bother you. When they occur, examine how they make you feel, and how the feeling influences your relationship. Discuss all this with your partner.
- Write "I am angry because...." Complete the sentence as rapidly as possible without thinking. Repeat it until you cannot come up with anything new. If you cannot think of anything, make up something. The truth will surface.
- Read the suggestions at the end of the chapter on anger.

12

Jealousy and Sex

Jealousy is a powerful emotion that can instigate cruelty, murder, and even suicide. Is it any wonder that it also can interfere with and destroy sexual pleasure?

Two types of jealousy can influence anyone's sex life. In the first, *inter*couple jealousy, one partner becomes jealous of the attention his or her mate gives to or receives from sources outside the relationship. (A common example is when a husband envies the attention his wife receives from friends or neighbors). This is what most people mean by jealousy. We tend to be less aware of *intra*couple jealousy, so called because the source and object of the jealousy lie *within* the relationship. The two common sources of jealousy within a relationship are (1) jealousy over sexual enjoyment, and (2) jealousy over previous partners. Both can affect sexual satisfaction.

INTRACOUPLE JEALOUSY

Jealousy Over Sexual Enjoyment
Most couples who suffer from this type of jealousy are not even aware that it exists. How can one partner's sexual joy

create problems? Are we not glad to see our partner have fun? Yes, most of the time we are happy when people we care about enjoy themselves. It is when one partner feels that the other *consistently* derives more pleasure from the sex act that problems arise.

We all want our fair share of the goodies; it is human nature to feel jealous when someone else always seems to get a bigger helping. The jealous partner begins to feel short-changed because the other is reaping all the benefits of "my hard work."

Jealousy over a partner's sexual enjoyment stems from the false belief that there is a limit to pleasure, that there is only so much enjoyment to go around. Thoughts such as "If my partner gets more than half of the fun, he/she is taking some of mine" are not just erroneous; they prevent the jealous part-

" SURE I ENJOY HAVING SEX WITH YOU. WHY, SOMETIMES IT'S SO GOOD IT'S ALL I CAN DO TO KEEP FROM LETTING YOU KNOW HOW FANTASTIC IT IS. "

ner from getting maximum pleasure. Too much time and effort
will be spent fighting for a fair share, worrying about cutting
up the pie instead of enjoying the feast. The net effect is to
lessen pleasure even more.

This type of jealousy is most apt to develop from one of three
situations.

1. *One partner is more expressive.* During sex expressive partners seem to exude ecstasy. Moans, groans, and other expressions of delight just pour forth. Silent partners may initially
enjoy this as a tribute to their own sexual prowess, but eventually they begin to feel jealous and resentful.

In reality, there is often no true difference between the partners' pleasure; one partner is simply more expressive and verbal about it. A problem develops only because the assumed
difference is not brought into the open and discussed. In some
cases this lack of communication has an ironic outcome.

James "snuck" into therapy without telling his wife. He felt
he had a serious sexual problem. He had sex often (at least
three times a week), but just did not enjoy it as much as he
"*should.*" The conversation went like this:

Therapist. How much should you enjoy it?
James. I don't know. More than I do. My wife loves it. I wish I
enjoyed it as much as she does.
Therapist. How much does she enjoy it?
James. I don't really know. She must enjoy it a whole lot.
Therapist. How's that?
James. Well, it's obvious! You know how it is when someone
really likes it.
Therapist. No, I don't. Tell me—how can you tell?
James. Well, . . . ah . . . you know, she makes lots of noises and
stuff.
Therapist. Go on.

What James described sounded like a very verbal, apprecia-
tive woman who was having a good time. We suggested he
bring her in for the next session. When he did he made an
amazing and ironic discovery.

Therapist. Can you tell Mable what those sounds mean to you.
James. Yeah. You're on cloud one hundred and nine! Overcome with pleasure!
Therapist. Can you be more specific about what *you're* feeling.
James. Well, I want to have as much fun. I feel you're getting more out of it than me.
Therapist. Mable, you look surprised.
Mable. You bet I am. The sounds help me to have a good time, sure, but . . . that's not what it's all about. I mean, . . . the first time I was noisy Jim here came at me like a tiger in heat. He loved it. At least I thought he did, judging by his reaction and all. Damn. I've been really letting it all come out 'cause I thought it was a turn-on for him. How embarrassing.

2. *One partner is too timid.* Sexual jealousy also arises when a partner does not ask for what he/she wants and needs to make sex more interesting or exciting. Many such individuals accept whatever comes their way. They do not have great expectations for sex, and get what they expect: "Okay sex, but nothing earth-shaking." Close examination of their sexual behavior reveals that they seldom, if ever, ask for special treatment.

Most probably have no idea what would make sex more exciting. They go through life never questioning their sex lives or level of pleasure. Usually it is their partner's seemingly intense pleasure that generates the suspicion that something is missing. Gradually, jealousy and resentment develop. Unfortunately, these timid individuals are usually reluctant to discuss their feelings and may even berate themselves for having such thoughts.

This happened to Mary Anne, a passive, accepting individual. She was sure that she had a sexual problem because her husband Jan enjoyed sex so much more than she. As we helped her examine her sex life, three things became clear: first, she had let her husband assume complete control over their sex life, never making suggestions or asking to have anything other than "missionary" sex; second, she believed that women are supposed to be passive; and third, she had been taught that sex is more fun for men than for women.

Mary Anne was aware that she felt jealous of her husband. This made her feel like a spoiled "child." The net effect was to make sex even less enjoyable, and she avoided it to keep from feeling jealous and evil. Once she adopted healthier attitudes she became more assertive. Her sex life improved "a thousand percent" and she no longer felt jealous or spoiled.

3. *Discrepant sex drives*. When partners experience a serious difference in sex drives, jealousy is apt to surface. The less active partner is likely to become resentful and jealous of the more active partner's obvious enjoyment. Remarks such as "That's all you think about!" "Do you ever wonder if there's something wrong with you because you like sex so much?" or "You have too many hormones!" indicate smoldering jealousy.

There are natural variations in sex drives. Occasionally, two individuals with a serious discrepancy become involved in a relationship. This discrepancy may be a genuine biological one (these cases are rare and should be resolved within the medical framework) or it may be a pseudo-discrepancy resulting from the infringement of nonsexual motives.

Pseudo-discrepancies should be examined from both the active and passive partners' perspectives because nonsexual motives may be operating for either or both. For example, the active partner may be trying to please, to earn self-esteem, or the like. The passive partner may be acting out of a lack of self-confidence, from repressed anger, or from some similar motive.

There is a third consideration: some people with "low sex drives" simply do not know what they want and have never explored what turns them on. When individuals with so-called "low sex drives" discover what they like and can do well, they experience a miraculous increase in sexual desire. This happened to Tina.

Tina thought she had a serious sexual problem. After one year of marriage her sex drive had "gone away." She explained that her husband wanted sex "much more often" than she did. Tina said she could take it or leave it, explaining, "It's not getting any better." The following exchange helped uncover her problem.

Therapist. Is sex good or bad for you?
Tina. Okay.
Therapist. But it's not getting any better?
Tina. No . . . but it should be, shouldn't it?
Therapist. What have you done to help it get better?
Tina. (perplexed) What do you mean? Am I supposed to do something special? Isn't it supposed to just get better the more you have it or something like that?
Therapist. Do you play any sports, or perhaps a musical instrument?
Tina. (more perplexed) Yes, but what does that have to do with sex?
Therapist. Well, . . .
Tina. (disgusted) I play tennis and the piano.
Therapist. Are you good at either? .
Tina. Well, I think so. Lots of people ask me to be their partner so I guess they like my game. And my husband likes to listen to me play the piano. In fact, he wants to buy us one. So . . . yes, I guess I'm pretty darn good. (annoyed) I still don't see what this has to do with my problem.
Therapist. How did you get so good?
Tina. At what? Tennis?
Therapist. Yes. Start with tennis.
Tina. I play a lot. I took a few lessons. In fact, I play every chance I get.
Therapist. Good. What about the piano?
Tina. Same, I guess. I practiced a lot when I was young. (smiles) My mother made me. But as I got older and learned to play better I enjoyed it more. Now I like to entertain myself and try new and different kinds of pieces.
Therapist. So it took a good deal of work and practice to get really good and to enjoy it as much as you do?
Tina. Sure. Isn't that the way it is with all things.
Therapist. Absolutely. Should sex be any different?
Tina. (dumbfounded) Sex? Work at sex? You aren't serious. I thought that was supposed to happen naturally.

Tina learned that sex was not getting any better for her

because sex does not just automatically improve. It takes practice to excel in any field. Sex is no exception. Yet everyone thinks it should be. This is the attitude behind most low sex drives: "I should be able to just lie back and enjoy." But if individuals do not explore, experiment, and practice, they do not give themselves the opportunity to discover the thousands of little pleasures that together make the big bang.

Jealousy Over Past Partners

This type of sexual jealousy is most common in second marriages or when one partner has had previous sexual experience. Less experienced partners become jealous of these previous affairs. Their insecurity leads them to conclude that they are not as good in bed as their more worldly partner. Men seem more susceptible to this pattern, perhaps as a holdover of the double standard, that women should be pure and chaste.

Working through this jealousy can lead to some very positive realizations. For example, after much soul-searching, Patricia stated it beautifully:

> I guess I feel I missed out on a very important part of his development, his early learning stage, when he was just discovering himself, his sex, his manliness, his body. I so wish I could have been there to share in it, to nurture it, to encourage it, to enjoy it. I feel I missed a charming, beautiful experience with him, and yes, I am jealous of those who were lucky enough to have had a part in it. I wish I could have been there, yet I know it's something that had to have happened before we met, otherwise "we" never would have happened. Our relationship just wouldn't be what it is and I wouldn't change or trade that for all of heaven and earth.

*   *   *

What can be done about intracouple jealousy?

- Adopt the attitude that there is always enough pleasure

to go around, that there is always room for more pleasure for each partner.

- Instead of worrying about how much your partner is enjoying sex, look for ways to increase your own pleasure. Ask yourself what you can do to make sex more interesting and pleasurable. If you are stuck, ask your partner to help you come up with ideas.
- Keep in mind that pleasure is a two-way street: the more you give, the more you get; the more you get, the more you can give. There is no limit to how pleasurable sex can be.
- If you feel underpleasured, ask for (if necessary, insist on getting) a full session of sex devoted exclusively to satisfying *your* whims and fantasies, where you decide who does what to whom or what you want done to you. Give you partner ample positive feedback on (a) how pleasurable the experience was for you; and (b) how skillfully he or she carried out your wishes.

INTERCOUPLE JEALOUSY

Most of us enjoy receiving attention from our partner. Most of us also feel threatened when we have to compete for that attention. Competition can arise from other people, inanimate objects (pictures, magazines), a career or hobby. Jealousy is a natural reaction to these intrusions.

We should express and discuss these feelings openly with our mate. If we do not, or if we try to deny them (even to ourselves), these feelings can have a profound effect on our sex lives.

Jealousy Over Attention from Others

We can react to intercouple jealousy in two ways: by (a) withholding sex in anger, or (b) seeking reassurance by demanding more sex. Michael chose the latter. Married to a very attractive younger woman, he would feel very insecure whenever another male showed any interest in his lover. At the first opportunity following this he would become very affectionate and seduce Barbara, his wife. Afterward he would solicit testimonials about his prowess. Initially, she did not connect his jealousy to his spectacular performance. She found his behavior cute and enjoyed his herculean efforts in bed.

One day Michael flew into a rage when he discovered that Barbara had been going out to lunch with a group from the office that included several men. He told her to dine with another group or skip eating. He then smiled at her and suggested going to bed.

When asked why he came for therapy he replied, "At that point she handed me my coat and told me to hit the road or the couch. I love her and can't give her up, so I came here."

Fortunately, Barbara realized the serious nature of Michael's jealousy and did not submit to his demands. She saved herself from a potentially miserable relationship and helped him too.

Jealousy Over Attention to Inanimate Objects

Jealousy can also be expressed by witholding sex, a pattern which Clare and Bill fell into. Bill enjoyed reading *Playboy* magazine, which upset Clare. She would refuse to have sex on any night she found him reading it. She reasoned, "I'm not going to let him find his pleasure with me. Let the one who started it finish the job."

Bill thought Clare's reaction was amusing but soon realized just how serious she was. She would refuse him sex if he so much as read the interview of the month. He decided to play along with her jealousy and told her that he had given up the magazine. Instead, he began to hide them and read them secretly. The couple sought therapy after Clare discovered Bill's hidden stack and became so angry that she burned the magazines and part of the basement carpet along with them.

Either jealous reaction—Clare's withholding sex or Michael's demanding it—is immature. Both create problems rather than solve them.

Jealousy Over Careers or Hobbies

It used to be that women were the exclusive victims of this type of jealousy. Men who might have felt jealous over a wife's career simply kept them at home with the children. Not any more. Today many men experience such jealousy.

The partner in competition with a career frequently makes increasing demands for attention. Sex is often used as the lure because of its assumed universal appeal and potency. As one person stated, "If sex doesn't work, what will?" However, sex is not an effective lure. The neglected partner is under pressure to make the act really worth it. The other partner is usually preoccupied with his/her career or hobby. Neither partner is relaxed, neither can focus on the sexual, and neither derives much pleasure and satisfaction from such engagements.

Unfortunately these situations are complicated by other factors. Individuals tend to become preoccupied with careers near middle life, just when it is common to experience a decline in sex drive. More unfortunately, mid-life is often an anxiety-laden time of reevaluation and readjustment. The mid-life crisis can only add to the tension of an unsatisfying sexual relationship. No one can enjoy sex under the pressure of competition over a career, a waning sex drive, and a mid-life crisis.

* * *

Such problems with jealousy are difficult to cure. The best cure is prevention, and the best prevention is to be forewarned and prepared:

- Develop a wide variety of interests so that you are not completely dependent on your partner for entertainment. Dependent people are more prone to bouts of intense jealousy.
- Cultivate friendships of your own so that you do not have to rely solely on your partner for companionship.
- With your mate, brainstorm for ways to lead a more

interesting life as a couple. What common interests can you develop and cultivate?

- Plan together for difficult times. Each should ask how the other plans to handle careers, jealousy, and so on.
- Continue to learn new things and develop personal assets. Remember that the best way to get your partner's attention is to be an interesting person. Lead a full life. Share your experiences. This is what keeps couples interested in each other.

13

Sex Motivated by Boredom

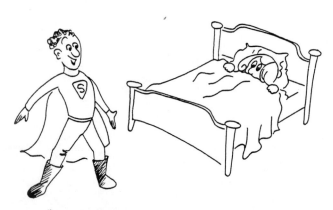

"LAST TIME YOU LOOKED BORED SO I THOUGHT I'D TRY SOMETHING DIFFERENT."

Mrs. P. came for therapy because she was disillusioned with marriage. Her husband was a real gem—easy to get along with, kind, considerate, and bright. The problem: she was bored out of her mind. All Mr. P. thought about was sex. He had no hobbies, no interests, no pastimes. Mrs. P. explained, "Oh, sex is great. He's really good. But, that's all he wants to do. He'll socialize if I initiate it. He'll go to a movie but doesn't care what kind. If I ask what he'd like to do it's always the same: Screw! Sex is fun. I like it. But there's got to be something else!"

Mrs. P. was absolutely right. No one should invest all of his or her time and interest in sex. Other areas must receive some attention as well. Sex simply cannot make up for what is lacking in the rest of our lives.

Mr. P. eventually came in to discuss his marriage, expressing surprise that his sex life had anything to do with his lack of hobbies. The therapist encouraged him to develop outside interests. To his amazement, sex improved. He capsulized it beautifully: "Now that I have other important things in my life I don't have to work so hard at sex. I can really relax and enjoy it."

Working is exactly what Mr. P. was doing. In order to avoid boredom he made a major production out of sex, making sure everything was just right: the music, the atmosphere, the lighting, and on and on. Furthermore, each time he had sex it had to be at least as good as the last time. As he said in therapy, "When sex is all you have it's got to be tops."

For many people the problem is not as serious. They simply have sex because they cannot think of anything better to do. They do not actively seek it; rather, it is their last choice, winning out by default. Is it any wonder that sex itself becomes boring, if there is no real interest in it to begin with? Individuals who use sex in this manner have not cultivated other interests, so they are "stuck" with going to bed.

Aaron and Jennifer had sex with reasonable frequency. Both felt it was "good" sex, but something was missing. After almost three years of marriage, they wondered if "that's all there is to it." Discussion revealed that Aaron and Jennifer led a rather boring life. Aside from some sports activity neither had any hobbies or interests.

Therapist. Well, what do you usually do? Describe a typical day, after work.

Aaron. We get home, relax, and eat (looks at Jennifer). Maybe we read the paper. (shrugs, looks at Jennifer for help) What else?

Jennifer. Watch TV whenever there's anything good, but that's rare.

Aaron. Once in a while we play volleyball or baseball. We belong to coed teams at work.

Therapist. Great! How often do you play?

Aaron. Well, whenever we get enough of the gang together, and weather permitting. I guess not all that often. I wish we could do it more.

Jennifer. Yeah, me too. I like to be active. Besides, it gives us something to do.

Therapist. What else do you folks do? (no response as Aaron and Jennifer look at each other; therapist looks at each) Well? With such busy lives, when on earth do you find time for sex? (Both laugh. Then Jennifer speaks.)

Jennifer. Ah . . . when there's nothing good on TV, and there's no game, and . . . I guess when we're all talked out, why, we just sort of go to bed.

Therapist. (exaggeratedly) Wow! Sounds like the ingredients for a real sizzler.

Aaron. Are you being sarcastic? If it gets any duller we'd fall asleep in the middle. . . .

Jennifer. Yeah! That's why we're here. Sex lacks a spark. It's boring before we even get started.

Therapist. That's exactly the problem. You are bored before you have sex.

Jennifer and Aaron. So what?

Therapist. If you watch TV because you're bored, what happens? If you play baseball because there's nothing else to do, do you play your best? Do you enjoy yourself?

Aaron. Of course not! But sex is different. It's supposed to be fun.

Therapist. Look! When is TV enjoyable? When there's a program you *want* to watch. When do you enjoy baseball most? When you *want* to play. When is anything most enjoyable? When you *want* to do it! Why should sex be any different? If you have sex because you *want* it, it *will* be fun. If you have it because you're bored, it can't possibly be as good. The point is, you're using sex to get rid of boredom. You're not seeking sex because you enjoy it. It gets dumped in your lap because you can't think of anything else to do. Under the circumstances, what do you expect from sex? An Olympic performance?

Jennifer. What can we do about it?

Aaron and Jennifer were instructed to forget about sex, or at least not to consider it a problem. Instead, they were to focus on nonsexual interests. Their assignment was for each to find and develop one area of individual interest and one area of joint interest.

Meanwhile, they met with the therapist every two or three weeks to discuss their progress and the problems involved in cultivating interests. In about six months both realized that a tremendous change had occurred. They had a much more interesting life outside the bedroom. They had sex more often and found it infinitely more enjoyable. Jennifer described their new situation: "We now have sex when we want it, and boy do we want it!"

This case reflects one of our key beliefs about sex, namely, that a healthy, interesting sex life develops out of a healthy interest in life and in one another. The more areas of interest partners have, the more opportunity they have to interact and to respond to each other on many levels. The spark of passion has ample opportunity to ignite and plenty of material to keep it going.

There is an old saying: "If you want something done, ask a busy person." In other words, busy people have many interests and find pleasure in many things; they always have room for one more project. This applies to sex as well. People who lead busy, interesting lives find ample time and opportunity for interesting sex. They are much too busy to use sex to alleviate or escape boredom. Rather, sex is a source of pleasure and enjoyment that they actively seek. They make time for sex. They do not expect it to fill the void in their leisure time.

" NO MOVIES. NOTHING ON T.V. NUTS!
WE MAY AS WELL HAVE SEX."

FEAR OF BOREDOM

Everyone wants to be considered a good, interesting bed partner. In fact, many people feel threatened that their spouses
may someday become bored with them sexually. This fear can
influence their present sexual behavior. Some people withhold
sex because they think that too much of a good thing is not
good, that the more you use something the less it will be enjoyed. These individuals or couples refrain from frequent sex
so they will not get bored. As one person put it, "My favorite
piece of music stays my favorite because I don't listen to it too
often."

Victims of this philosophy fail to realize that withholding
sex *creates* boredom. By withholding sex, opportunities to ex-

plore new facets of sexual enjoyment and expand sexual horizons are limited.

Sex is not a commodity that wears out or gets used up. It
has an infinite number of angles to be explored. (See Chapter
22.) If couples do not have sex regularly, they cannot appreciate
the full range of sexual responses, the thousands of nuances,
associations, and sensations that create the richness of human
sexuality. In simple terms, they get bored with sex when they
have only routine, superficial intercourse without exploring or
using their imaginations. They are rigid bed partners, and
chances are the bedroom situation reflects the rest of their
lives.

THE BOREDOM AFFAIR

We must not overlook the individuals who, bored in their
present sexual relationship, seek outside entertainment. Certainly an affair can bring excitement into a boring life. But
why is this person bored to begin with?

Behind every static sex life lurk nonsexual problems that
contribute to the boredom that leads to the affair. When these
nonsexual needs are resolved, interest in the affair subsides.

The dynamics of boredom affairs can be quite complicated,
as in Janice and Bart's case. They came for therapy to try to
save their marriage. Bart had discovered that Janice was having an affair with Mike, a co-worker, whom Bart thought was
a "silly twit." In therapy Janice admitted she was bored with
sex, that Bart was rigid and entirely too serious in bed. She
just wanted to have fun, and Mike seemed to fill the bill with
his incessant clowning in and out of the bedroom.

From the start, Janice had hesitated to discuss the problem
with Bart because she was afraid there was something wrong
with her. By having the affair she hoped to confirm that she
was still sexy. As she talked, Janice also learned that she was

afraid to experiment because "I didn't know where it would lead." In fact, she was afraid to explore her own sexuality. Both of these fears contributed to her choosing a silly, immature individual as a partner in the affair.

Bart had many misconceptions about sex. He believed that sex is "serious business" because it is "what holds couples together. . . . It separates the men from the boys." He added, "Men have got to be considerate of a lady's every need." No wonder he could not relax and have fun in bed! Once these issues were discussed and resolved, Janice and Bart rediscovered each other in the bedroom. Neither had any further interest in an affair.

There is nothing wrong with having sex when you are bored if it is done on an occasional basis. Sex may temporarily alleviate boredom. Unfortunately, it can easily become a habit which, in the long run, will make sex less fulfilling and prevent you from developing other interests and skills. Instead, lead an interesting, full life and your sex life will follow suit.

The suggestions on page 96 apply here as well.

14

Sex for Dominance and Control

The idea of dominating other people and controlling their behavior is not new. Blackmail, corporate spying, international intrigue, and espionage are obvious examples. In intimate relationships, many individuals use sex for control on a more subtle level.

The behavior that one partner wants to control in the other is called the target behavior. Sometimes the target behavior is not specific. The goal is to prevent change in the relationship by preventing a mate's growth and independence. One partner is very insecure and immature and views change or growth in the other as a threat. Any attempt to step beyond the "couple mentality" is discouraged and squelched.

It is easy to fall into the trap of using sex to keep the errant partner in line, as Paul and Ann found out. Paul was low man on the totem pole at work. Socially, he had few friends, and felt generally uncomfortable in group situations. He never felt in charge. He married Ann, a quiet, traditional woman, and made his home his castle. Ann seemed only too glad for Paul to be in command, at least in the beginning.

Occasionally Ann expressed a desire to join an organization, take classes, get a part-time job, or otherwise develop some independence. Paul panicked at these suggestions, fearing that he would lose Ann, the only thing in his life he controlled. His reaction was to head for the bedroom, literally seducing Ann into not following through with her plans.

Ann was controlled in this manner for about eight months, after which she began to see through Paul's tactics. She gave this account of Paul's behavior: "Every time I plan to go some-where or do something, that's the day Paul will come home with special wine or flowers or with reservations at an expen-sive restaurant. Every time it's 'Oh, I forgot!' Sometimes he gets nasty and claims I'm ruining our sex life. If I stay home I can't enjoy sex. I feel patronized. If I leave I feel guilty all evening."

In therapy Paul worked through his fear of Ann changing and searched for new ways to gain control over his life. Had they not come for therapy he would have remained a frightened, dominating husband, and Ann might have developed into a frustrated houseplaymate without any interests, skills, or con-fidence. If their relationship were to go sour in later years, Ann probably would be left in a socially and economically helpless state.

In this case Paul attempted to use sex to control Ann but Ann refused to cooperate in these transactions. All too often both partners collude to foster dependency in each other and prevent individual growth. The tactics involved are subtle. Neither partner is aware of the effects of their interaction.

These couples believe they are building a solid, intimate relationship. They function as if a couple were a single unit instead of two individuals with separate identities. They have the same friends, interests, and opinions or beliefs. At parties they socialize as a unit, frequently kissing and winking and literally hanging onto each other. They seem inseparable, like "twins," and are often the envy of less unified couples.

In fact, "twin couples" are very insecure. The clinging behavior is designed to keep each focused exclusively on the other. The public romantic behavior is a semi-sexual lure, a constant reminder to each other that "I am ready any time you are." With such a powerful lure, there is no room for other interests to develop. Their attention remains riveted on each other.

These couples tend to remain at the same level of development for several years. During this time they feel that they are deeply in love and that everything between them is just wonderful. In fact, their relationship is static, with neither one growing or maturing. As the relationship ages the aura of romance fades, conflict and strife set in, and the "unity" deteriorates rapidly. Friends are always shocked at the news of their separation.

Bob and RoseAnn were such a couple. Before marriage they were always arm-in-arm at every social function. Everyone thought they were the ideal couple. After marriage they were literally inseparable. At parties they only separated to get drinks or go to the bathroom, always parting with a wink and a kiss. Everyone just adored them. Everyone thought Bob and RoseAnn must have a hot sex life and could not live without each other.

This went on for over four years. All their friends were dumbfounded when Bob and RoseAnn suddenly decided to separate. Bob and RoseAnn had, at best, a mediocre relationship and sex life. The public display of romance and the constant hint of powerful sexual attraction were seldom genuine. These tactics simply served as a lure to keep the two partners focused on each other. The subtle message was "Don't get interested in anything. I'm here to serve your every need." Thus they succeeded in keeping each other from becoming mature, well-rounded individuals—using sex to stifle individuality and independence.

SPECIFIC TARGET BEHAVIOR

In the last two cases sex was used to foster dependency. Often it is used to control a more specific target behavior. Such was the case for Suzanne and Julio. Julio was not a heavy drinker, but he did like to stop for a drink after work. Suzanne resented Julio's spending money on alcohol, especially his buying a round for his buddies. Suzanne could not tolerate the behavior, but was reluctant to bring the matter up. Once she complained mildly, and Julio replied, "Why don't you come down and join me? I'd really like that."

This was not the reply Suzanne had hoped for. She wanted Julio to come straight home. Inadvertently, she began attempting to control his behavior through sex. When Julio came home from the bar feeling romantic Suzanne responded with a cold shoulder; if Julio came home early, without stopping for a drink, Suzanne enticed him into passionate love-making.

After several months Julio figured out this pattern in their sex life. He felt manipulated, not knowing if Suzanne's passionate love plays were genuine. He doubted her sincerity, began to avoid sex, and spent more time at the bar.

Thus Suzanne lost her source of control, and in turn began to doubt Julio's love for her. At this point, therapeutic intervention helped both see clearly how Suzanne used sex as a control device. They discussed her discomfort with Julio's after-work behavior and came to a compromise which pleased both.

In a sense Suzanne tried to make a trade-off with Julio. She was willing to give sex if Julio would return directly home from the office. The trade was neither openly stated nor mutually agreed upon. However, some couples do barter openly and succesfully with sex, as described in the next section.

SEX AS BARTER

Neither of the two types of barter we consider here is harmful in and of itself. However, both can lead to problems. The first type is the more benign: exchanging sexual favors.

Exchanging Sexual Favors

Exchanging sexual favors, a very common practice, usually takes the form "I'll do this to you if you'll do that to me," or "Let's have it this way now. Next time we'll do it your way." Many couples barter and enjoy it. There is nothing harmful about this practice; it can actually enhance a relationship. However, if sexual barter is made to function for nonsexual reasons, it detracts from sexual pleasure. Problems are created when the trade is not openly stated. This is precisely why Al and Margaret ran into problems.

Al was somewhat bashful and reluctant to ask for what he wanted. He would simply do Margaret's favorites, hoping she would get the hint and reciprocate. This seldom happened because Margaret assumed that Al must be doing what he wanted. "After all," Margaret said, "he never suggested anything else." Al built up considerable resentment and began avoiding sex because "Marge always gets what she wants. I always feel frustrated."

Al's hidden motive was to please himself. He did not succeed so he felt frustrated and unsatisfied. Had he told Margaret what he wanted, there would have been no hidden motive—and no problem. Obviously, the cure in such cases is for partners to simply state what they want.

Bartering can be fun when it's open, fair, and enjoyable to both partners and when each partner follows through on any promises. But if a couple can only have sex through excessive or compulsive bartering, something else may be wrong. Furthermore, serious problems can arise when it is time to repay favors. If either partner continually indulges in sex to repay favors yet derives little or no pleasure from the repayment, sexual enthusiasm and satisfaction will take a nose dive. Thus both partners must be well aware of what the deal is and what effect it has on their sex life.

Exchanging Sex for Nonsexual Favors

Some individuals use sex to gain favors outside the bedroom. Examples are: "If we eat out I'll be in a very loving mood"; "If we go to see *Dr. Zhivago* instead, I'll be more romantic"; or "I find the mountains more romantic than the shore. How about spending our vacation there?"

Again, there is potential here for serious problems. When the object is to control your mate and get your way, without regard to the pleasure and satisfaction of *both* partners, then barter is being used for hidden motives—with negative side effects.

Barter works only when it is done openly and neither party feels coerced. A vacation in the mountains can be very enjoyable to both. The fact that one partner becomes more amorous in a certain atmosphere can certainly add to the vacation. But if the proposition were stated "I hate the shore! No mountains, no sex!" there would be no choice and sex would be used to gain control. Likewise, saying "If I cook—no sex," or "We eat out or no sex," is not an exchange; it is an ultimatum. The controlling partner may get his/her way but, in the long run, the sex life will suffer. These ultimatums resemble conditional sex, discussed below, which is another method of controlling a partner's behavior in the bedroom.

CONDITIONAL SEX

In conditional sex one partner controls the sexual behavior of both. There are no exchanges involved: it is sex on one partner's terms or no sex at all. This is surprisingly common, but most couples are not aware that the pattern exists in their relationship.

Edna and Greg were such a couple. They came for therapy because their sex life had ground to a halt. Neither understood how this had happened because initially their sex life had been wonderful. In therapy they discovered the hidden pattern in their sexual relationship. Edna feared that Greg was excessively sexual, so she continually put greater stipulations on their bedroom encounters. At first Greg did not care and was ready for sex under any conditions. Gradually, however, he found Edna more and more difficult to arouse. He explained, "Turning Edna on is like warming up an elephant. I just don't enjoy it any more."

Sex therapy consisted of each of them making a list of what they found pleasurable. Then they were to take turns doing each other's favorites until they established a natural, comfortable frequency. After three months they lost track of who did what to whom for how long and how often. Their sex life charted its own course and both were satisfied.

This is the typical pattern of conditional sex. Initially the more aggressive, eager partner tolerates any stipulation the less eager partner places on their encounters. Eventually, however, the eager partner loses enthusiasm and withdraws. The other partner succeeds not only in controlling the eager one's sex drive but in extinguishing it all together.

There is some similarity between conditional sex and sex for atonement. In both cases one partner becomes the workhorse of the bedroom. However, in sex for atonement the workhorse takes responsibility for the pleasure and satisfaction of both, finally losing interest in sex because he or she begins to feel sexually incompetent: pleasing the other partner becomes impossible. In conditional sex the eager partner is out for a good time, for self-pleasure, with no concern about pleasing the other. The goal is simply to have fun. This workhorse does not accept the role of pleaser and loses interest in sex only because it is no longer fun.

No one should control or try to control someone else's sex drive. Couples must work out the logistics of satisfying, not limiting or squelching, both parties' sexual needs.

Dorothea and Emilio ran into problems because they did not

follow this advice. They came to therapy because Emilio had lost his sex drive. He had changed, according to Dorothea, from a tiger to a pussycat. She suspected he ran around with other women.

As we discussed their sex life, the following pattern surfaced. Both liked sex. Dorothea enjoyed it most when her man came at her like an animal and she had found a way to get Emilio to do just that. During foreplay she would make remarks that reflected on Emilio's ability as a lover: "Any wimp can do that. Show me what a real man can do," or "Kiss me like a man, not a little boy." Emilio would become angry and turn into the aggressive tiger Dorothea wanted.

She was satisfied and got her way. Emilio enjoyed the intense sex, but felt uncomfortable and unsatisfied because of the unresolved anger that Dorothea provoked during foreplay. Even-

"BUT DEAR, I GO TO BED WITH OTHER MEN FOR YOUR OWN GOOD. THAT WAY IT WILL TAKE LONGER FOR ME TO GET BORED WITH YOU."

tually the unsatisfied anger overpowered the sexual satisfaction and pleasure. He began to avoid sex completely.

Dorothea paid a high price for getting her way in the bedroom. Discussing her desires and being willing to alternate her needs with Emilio's would have kept the problem from occuring. It is natural to want your own way in sexual matters. But discussion and compromise will lead to satisfaction for both partners.

* * *

Individuals most likely to use sex to control others are those who:

- are rigid and feel threatened by change.
- do not have faith in their ability to adapt to growth in their partner.
- feel helpless and out of control in other areas of their lives.
- disregard the feelings and needs of others.

What can you do if you discover such a pattern in your relationship?

- Do not panic. Take inventory of your interests, skills, and talents; then develop your own strengths; cultivate a hobby. Insecure people who try to control each other usually have not developed their own interests, talents, or strengths.
- Encourage your partner to do the same. Otherwise, he or she will undermine your efforts toward self-development.
- Express these concerns to your partner as they arise. Do not let anxieties gnaw away at you.
- Never try to solve any problem or correct your partner's behavior—drinking, continually working late at the

office, whatever it may be—through sex. It will usually backfire. Discuss the problem behavior openly and resolve it without any recourse to the bedroom.

As far as specific bedroom behavior is concerned, remember this point from earlier discussion: no one partner should always be the boss or the workhorse. If you are unhappy about your role in the bedroom, discuss your feelings with your mate. Here are some additional suggestions:

- Reverse roles in the bedroom. Discuss how the new role feels, its advantages and disadvantages, and how much you liked or disliked it. A compromise can easily arise out of such a discussion.
- Create a joint fantasy and act it out. If either partner disagrees, take turns completing the fantasy. Trade off being the director. Discuss how each of you felt. Reverse roles in the fantasy and repeat. You may wish to save the replay for another time.
- Try something new. Have a novelty night during which both partners do something they have never tried before. Discuss your reactions to the event. Reverse roles. Discuss again.

15

Sex as a Haven

Don and Melinda, both teachers, arrived home at the same time each day. They headed straight for the bedroom and became lost in the heat of passion. After two years of this daily ritual, sex had become dull. It was their daily cocktail, relaxing them after a nerve-racking day of unruly kids and unreasonable administrators. As Don stated, "It's gotten so that I can't even think until after sex. On weekends we don't have sex. We don't seem to need it." Melinda agreed: "I don't think either one of us really enjoys it as sex anymore. I can't do without it, yet I don't enjoy it."

Neither could recall exactly how it all started, but both agreed that initially they had felt rejuvenated after sex, "like we could get on with the rest of our day." Don and Melinda did not really enjoy teaching. Sex was a signal that the bad part of the day was over.

In therapy they saw that they were using sex as an escape, a release from tension and stress, a balm for an unsatisfying career—as everything but a source of sexual pleasure and satisfaction. No wonder they both felt totally frustrated! With all these nonsexual needs to satisfy, there was no room for sexual pleasure.

A similar problem developed for Bernie and Dusty, who operated a small printing and advertising business. There were always deadlines to meet, corrections to make, and disgruntled customers to satisfy. Whenever the day became chaotic they escaped into the bedroom for their "tasty-cake break." At first this tactic worked: both felt rejuvenated and attacked their problems with renewed vigor. Eventually, however, sexual frustration surfaced. Their excursions into the bedroom became disasters that added to their problems. Yet they were unable to stop using sex in this manner. They did not know how else to calm themselves down.

These are typical cases of couples who habitually use sex as a "martini"—a haven or escape. Through sex they seek to rejuvenate their worn spirits or alleviate nonsexual tension and stress. Sex thus acquires an entirely new role, that of nurturer, stabilizer, or relaxer.

These cases demonstrate three important points about using sex as a haven. First, it almost always works in the beginning. The couple or individual *does* find solace in sex. Second, it becomes habit-forming, and the cycle is very difficult to break. Even when the couple is aware of the problem they cannot seem to stop. Third, the real problem is that the couple lacks a nonsexual solace or relaxant. Once they find one they will be free to pursue true sexual pleasure, and their sex lives will automatically improve.

Sometimes only one partner uses sex as an escape or solace. In these cases problems surface more quickly. The partner misusing sex will want it at inappropriate times. The other partner will sense this misuse and very soon will find sex frustrating and oppressive. Often this partner feels used, as happened to Rhonda.

Rhonda complained that she did not enjoy sex with her husband. He usually wanted it soon after he arrived home from the office. According to Rhonda, "He wants to get in bed before he finishes his martini. I want to get out as fast as I can." As she discussed her dissatisfaction it became clear that Rhonda felt used. "Well, I guess I feel like I'm his second martini. I'm there to spread my legs and get rid of his tension from the office just so he can get to the paperwork he brought home."

Rhonda's husband resisted therapy. Sam would not come in to discuss the problem, insisting instead on his conjugal rights. The problem was solved with a little careful planning. Rhonda was instructed to place a martini, a note, and the newspaper next to her husband's easy chair, and leave just before he arrived home. When she returned he was in a more relaxed mood. Sam was amazed at how much better sex was when he did not use it to unwind or to take a break from stressful work.

Sam's refusal to participate in therapy is not unusual. Such individuals are often satisfied with their sex life. Their attitude is that "You're the dissatisfied one, so it's your problem." They may also be afraid that sex will change for the worse. This rarely happens. Usually there is an immediate improvement in sex for both partners. Sex is always better when stress and tension are at a minimum.

* * *

Individuals most likely to use sex as a "martini" are those who:

- are generally tense and cannot relax.
- must always be doing something productive and have no hobbies or interests other than work.
- lead unsatisfying lives and have stressful, unsatisfying jobs.

If you are one of these individuals, what can you do to relax?

- Take a vacation and take stock of your life, your job, and your relationship. Look for sources of stress and ways you can cope with them.

- Do nothing but watch the clouds roll along. Focus on the simple benefits of life that surround you but that you normally overlook.
- Unwind *before* you have sex. Try deep muscle relaxation or meditation before you enter the bedroom.
- Listen to music: classical and instrumental styles can be very soothing.
- Take up a vigorous sport or exercise regularly.
- Take a course or read a book on stress management.
- Plan a weekend vacation at home. Set aside a Saturday or Sunday as the day you and your mate will do nothing unpleasant or stressful. You must plan your day; for example,

  8 A.M.–11 A.M. Relax in bed with humorous books, video tapes, or the like.

  11:30–to 1:30. Go out to brunch.

  2:00–3:00. Take a leisurely walk.

  3:00–3:45. Read to each other.

  Evening. Plan on dancing, dinner, a show. Then have sex and notice the difference when it is not used to alleviate stress.

16

Sex and Social Pressure

Humans are social animals. We pay close attention to others—how they eat, talk, dress, and behave. What other people say or do inevitably affects our own behavior. This phenomenon is called social pressure, and it enters all facets of our lives, including the bedroom.

How does social pressure influence sexual behavior? Simply knowing what others do in the bedroom increases the chances that we will do likewise. This in not a new idea. Serious concern over publishing sexual data has been expressed by many behavioral and social scientists.

How can just knowing what others do in the bedroom affect our sexual behavior? There are two plausible explanations.

    1. When we read sexual data we compare our behavior to the published norms. If there is a discrepancy we assume that something is wrong with us. Consequently, we adjust our activity toward the norm.

    2. Most of us have fantasies about sexual acts, but we are reluctant to try them. Generally we do not even

talk about them because we are not sure if such acts are socially acceptable. When we read that others do them, our fantasies seem more normal and we are more likely to try them.

Sex data are not the only way we learn what others are doing. Television and movies also influence our perception of what is normal. They literally bombard us with cheating couples, risqué or casual sex, and sex to manipulate others. We could easily get the impression that everyone is doing everything to everybody.

The more often we see different sexual behaviors on the screen, the more normal or widespread we believe they are. After the movie *Four Seasons,* for example, many people inquired about the normality of slapping or spanking during sex, and of May–September relationships. The following cases also show how social pressure can influence our sex lives.

Mr. and Mrs. J called for an appointment because they felt they had a serious sex problem. For years they had been having sex about once a week. Recently, they read a survey that said the national average was 2.3 times per week. The J's did not want to be abnormal, so they increased their frequency. Much to their dismay, it became less enjoyable. They were sure something was wrong with them.

In fact, everything was fine. With their therapist they discussed individual variations in sexual needs and how nonsexual motives—such as trying to meet national norms—lessen sexual pleasure. The J's were instructed to forget about national norms, follow their own needs, and call back if any problems developed. About two months later Mrs. J called to report that everything was fine. She and her husband had decided that sex once a week afforded them the greatest amount of pleasure and satisfaction, "national norms be damned."

This case, while mild in nature, illustrates a very important point: Sex to keep up with the Joneses (or the national averages) is not likely to yield much personal pleasure and satisfaction. However, not all social pressure on sex is negative. Sometimes it can be beneficial, which is exactly how it affected Ron and Terry.

After two years of marriage, Terry wanted to try oral sex. Ron was shocked. He had been raised by stern grandparents who thought that everything but missionary sex was immoral. Terry convinced him to experiment after showing him a survey indicating that over 50% (her figures) of their peers enjoyed oral sex. Their problem: both liked it, but Ron would seldom indulge. He felt perverted because he liked it so much. Ron had to develop his own moral code to include his newly discovered pleasure.

Other common examples of social pressure influencing sexual behavior are:

- the married individual who never considered an affair until reading that over 50% of the married wander —suddenly it does not seem like such a bad idea.
- the individual who has sex simply because *everyone* else does.
- the 23-year-old virgin who indulges because others will suspect he/she is strange.
- the couple who try swinging or an open marriage because they read so much about it becoming acceptable.

Obviously, we do not live in a vacuum. So to what extent should we be influenced by what others do? What role should sexual data play in our sex lives? On one hand, we could become social isolates, completely free of other people. Or, we could let others dictate our actions completely, by deciding what is pleasurable or normal based on statistical data or other outside influences. Neither extreme is wise.

The answer is this: We should never do anything sexual just because everyone, someone, or no one is doing it. We should do what we want, when we want, because it is pleasurable to our partners and ourselves. Social norms and statistical data should serve as a stimulus for thought about our own behavior and beliefs. For example, if the national average is 2.3 times per week and a couple has sex bi-annually, maybe something is wrong. Likewise, if 90% of all married people have sex in several positions and a couple still insists on missionary sex in the dark, maybe it is time they reexamined their attitudes and beliefs. But we should not assume that what most people do is automatically right or good. Suppose 60% of all married couples have affairs; this does not mean that having an affair is good or right for you. Or, suppose 60% of all couples indulge in S and M; this does not mean that you should do the same the next time you have sex. These hypothetical statistics illustrate just how absurd such reasoning would be.

* * *

Individuals most likely to be highly influenced by social pressures are those who:

- do not have clearly defined personal standards.
- judge themselves by what others think and do.
- were raised by strict parents and rebelled but did not establish a personal code of ethics.
- are adolescents.

What can you do to minimize the effect of social pressure on your sex life?

- Think through your own sexual code of ethics. What is right or wrong for you? Examine how you came to your beliefs. Are your reasons mature and logical or are they born of a TV fantasyland or a fire and brimstone fanaticism. If your reasons are of the latter origin, consult the chapters on guilt, rebellion, and self-esteem. If your code of ethics is from fantasyland, you probably have many nonsexual motives influencing your sex life. Complete the questionnaire on page 181 and consult the appropriate chapters.

- If your partner wants you to do something you feel is repulsive or weird, stick to your own judgment until you can consult a reputable, licensed, clinical psychologist or sex therapist. They are usually happy to discuss such issues.
- Keep an open mind about what is normal. Our rule of thumb: the act or the frequency of the act (1) should be enjoyable to both partners, (2) should not be mentally or physically harmful, and (3) should not lower self-esteem or stimulate guilt.
- When in doubt about statistics or an act you would like to experience, try this: on one side of a sheet of paper write down everything your parents would say about it. Turn the sheet over and write down what you think a liberal person would say. Then take a new sheet of paper and write down what *you* feel is right. Chances are you are somewhere in between the two extremes. Now consider each point on each list. Argue and compromise. Finally, on a new sheet of paper, write the conclusions you have reached. Do this every week or two for several weeks. Note how your beliefs evolve to precise conclusions.
- If you have trouble with the exercise above, try this: Divide a sheet of paper into two columns. In one column jot down all the reasons for indulging. In the other column list all the reasons for refraining. Next, decide if each pro and con is logical (appeals to your reason) or emotional. Separate the emotional items from the logical ones. Debate each emotional reason until you reach some resolution or compromise. Repeat this sev-

eral times over several weeks. You will arrive at a resolution comfortable to you.

"I CAN'T DECIDE WHAT TO DO THIS SATURDAY. GO OUT WITH HORNIE HARRY OR SEE CHAIN SAW MASSACRE FOR THE SEVENTH TIME."

17

Sex as a Buffer for Depression

Sex used as a buffer against depression can develop out of a couple's patterns of interaction and sexual response. Or, it can result from the individual's personality dynamics. We will begin with the former: couples using sex to alleviate depression.

No one likes to feel sad or be around a sad person. It is difficult to keep our own spirits up when people we love feel down. The normal reaction is to cheer them up, by offering trite advice: "Look at the bright side!" "You need a stiff drink"; or, unwittingly, by recommending sex as a way to prevent depression.

It happens like this: One partner feels down. The other becomes solicitous. A few understanding words of consolation, an affectionate hug, a few kisses, and before either is aware of it they are having sex. Both feel better afterwards; neither is down in the dumps. In effect, they have just used sex to alleviate depression.

This is exactly what happened to Joan and Roger. They came for therapy uncertain what their problem was. Finally, a comment made by Joan uncovered the issue.

Joan. I don't know! I really don't! All I know is that sex doesn't
make me feel good any more.
Therapist. Make you feel good?
Joan. Yeah. Sex used to be great! I'd feel good after it was over.
I'd be cheerful and happy. . . . It made my day!
Therapist. So sex was a pick-up, like a cup of coffee when you
can't get going in the morning.
Joan. Yeah. It really works . . . well, it used to. No matter what
was bothering me before, after sex it didn't phase me.

Joan and Roger found that they were using sex to avoid
dealing with Joan's sadness, heading for the bedroom instead
of discussing what was bothering her. In therapy they learned
how to help each other explore and resolve unpleasant, sad
feelings. They also discovered how much more pleasurable sex
is when it is not used to alleviate sadness.

Similar patterns occur in many marriages. One partner feels
sad; the other becomes nurturant and tries to cure the sadness
with sex. The end result: sadness is temporarily relieved, but
sex is mediocre. No one can experience full sexual ecstasy with
depression lurking at the bedroom door.

The depression must be dealt with before sex. Once the source
of the sad feeling is discovered and resolved, the couple can go
on to sex if they so desire. Sex after a couple shares and works
through some intimate problem is infinitely more satisfying.

Repeatedly using sex as a buffer against depression can have
serious repercussions:

1. The couple's sex life becomes geared toward negative
   feelings. They learn to respond sexually to sad, unpleasant feelings. They are also teaching one another
   to act sad when sex is desired.
2. Couples may learn to need and use each other and sex
   only to ward off depression. Eventually, their relationship may function entirely as an anti-depressant,
   their lives consisting of a recurring threat of depression

kept in abeyance by sex. If the couple no longer needs an anti-depressant, they will no longer need each other. They may lose their sexual attraction for one another and their relationship will seem meaningless.

This is what happened to Bill and Josephine. After five years of marriage they decided to call it quits. As Bill put it, "We don't love each other. I'm not even sure we like each other. Neither of us can figure out why we got together in the first place." Josephine agreed, lamenting that they used to like and need each other and get along respectably.

A review of their early family experiences, courtship, and marriage uncovered the problem. Both had unhappy, poverty-stricken childhoods. Both were mistreated by their parents. One could only conclude that they were very depressed adolescents who found counsel and solace in each other. As they became sexually involved they learned to use sex as their anti-depressant. When either looked depressed or sad, the other would become solicitous and caring. They would inevitably end up in bed.

Shortly after marriage they found lucrative, satisfying jobs. Their lives changed. Both became carefree individuals, their depression subsiding as their self-esteem grew. They no longer needed each other or sex to ward off depression. Neither one could find any reason to continue the marriage.

Couples who are excessively dependent on each other for happiness are most likely to use sex as an anti-depressant. Dependent individuals will frequently make statements such as "You are the only spark of sunshine in my life," "You are my reason for living," "I couldn't live without you," and so on. But happiness is an emotional experience that must come from within, not from another person.

Also, couples who cannot openly face and discuss negative feelings, events, and situations tend to seek sex as an anti-depressant. Everyone has negative, unpleasant feelings that must be accepted and dealt with; otherwise sex can easily be misused.

Thus far we have seen that couples can collaborate to use sex as an anti-depressant. Next we shall consider the general relationship between sex and depression in the individual.

SEX AND DEPRESSION

Sex has value as an anti-depressant because of the nature of sex and the way it interacts with an individual's personality dynamics. There is a surprising and complex relationship between sex and depression. Seriously depressed individuals feel sad, isolated, unwanted, unneeded, and/or helpless. They typically feel they cannot do anything to help themselves. Their appetite is poor; they do not sleep well; nothing seems to give them pleasure. They lose interest in everything—*including sex*. As we would expect, there is little or no sexual activity and even less sexual pleasure.

However, the surprise comes in the early stages of depression, which some clinicians refer to as the pre-inception stage. During this stage sexual activity increases. Depressed individuals become more interested in sex. It seems to become more pleasurable than usual. They frequently report that sex is getting better or has never been so good. Many clinicians have observed that sex seems, at least temporarily, to prevent depression.

How can sex possibly hold back depression? There are five major explanations:

1. The intensity and pleasure of the sex act counteracts the emotional deadness building up inside. Sex is like a ray of sunshine focusing attention away from the approaching depression.
2. Sex necessitates contact with another person. This brings temporary relief from the emerging emotional

isolation that accompanies depression. Again, attention is focused away from depressed feelings.

3. Theoretically, depression is anger and aggression turned inward. Sex involves aggressive behavior, and affords the opportunity to direct some of the repressed aggression and anger outward. The result is a temporary respite from the effects of the repressed feelings.

4. People who get depressed suffer a loss of self-esteem. Sex can be used to earn self-esteem (see Chapter 8).

5. Most individuals who use sex as an anti-depressant seem to have had an unhappy childhood and adolescence. They learned to find relief in masturbation; now they have a partner. These individuals tend to be preoccupied with sex—focusing on it to avoid facing the depression.

Of course, sex can provide only minor, temporary relief from depression. The sad feelings will eventually surface and take their course. However, some individuals succeed in holding back depression with sex for remarkably long periods, as the following case illustrates.

Joe, a bright man of 28, came for therapy because of a recurring nightmare. He could not recall what it was about, but each night for the last two months he had awakened startled and tight-faced, "as if I were ready to burst out crying." Recently, his wife woke him because he was sobbing hysterically in his sleep. He could not recall the dream or why he was crying. At his wife's encouragement he came for help.

Joe described his life as happy. He had been married almost four years and was very pleased with his situation. "My wife makes me feel on top of the world," he reported. Their sex life seemed very good until the dreams began. "We both love sex, especially me. There's just nothing better in the universe," Joe stated emphatically. For the last four or five months, however, Joe had been feeling that something was missing. He had no idea what it could be.

With the aid of hypnosis Joe was able to recall his dream. It was of a little boy being whipped by a masked figure, dressed in a black gown. Unmasking the figure—his father—unleashed a torrent of anger and resentment. Joe told of his unbelievably cruel father who had teased and beaten him unmercifully until Joe was 12. Joe's father died at that point.

Joe recounted that he was a miserable human being until about age 18, when he dicovered girls and what a good lover he was. Everything seemed fine. He worked his way through college determined not to be the "bastard" his father had been. By the time he met Liz, his wife, he had "forgotten" about his terrible past. Liz, and sex, became the center of his universe. Everything was wonderful: he was on his way to becoming president of his company; he and Liz married and were blissfully happy. It was when Liz announced her pregnancy that the dreams began and sexual interest and enjoyment waned. The coming child began to stir up memories of Joe's own childhood.

In this case, women and sex became the buffer against severe depression. Joe managed remarkably well considering his early life experiences, but in the end the depression surfaced. This case was complicated by his father's cruelty and death, but nonetheless demonstrates the connection between sex and depression.

For most individuals the problem is not as severe; nor is the connection between sex and depression so obvious. Nonetheless, our sex lives are affected by our emotional state. When we are at peace with ourselves and others, sex is genuinely pleasurable and satisfying. When we are down, sex can easily be used as a crutch or bastion against depression. As always, when sex is used for nonsexual purposes our level of satisfaction is affected.

* * *

Individuals most likely to use sex to avoid or alleviate depression are those who:

- Try to repress or deny unpleasantness. Their motto is "Keep a stiff upper lip in the face of adversity." Instead of facing the negative feelings and dealing with the bad situations, they try to avoid or negate them.
- Are preoccupied with sex.
- Had unhappy early lives and stern parents.

The best cure for depression is to stop fighting it and let it surface. Only then can it be resolved. Depression only influences your sex life when you and/or your partner deny its existence.

Couples can prevent sex from being used as an anti-depressant by:

- Discussing sadness and helpless feelings as they arise. Do not give trite advice or insist on focusing on the positive. Help your partner by: (a) acknowledging the unpleasant feelings; (b) sharing similar feelings and incidents; (c) looking, together, for ways the sad or helpless partner can correct the situation.
- Never trying to talk your partner out of feeling sad or helpless. The feelings will only resurface later.
- Recognizing that repressed anger often leads to depression. It may help to look for recent events or situations that angered you but which you were unable to resolve when they occurred.
- Reading the suggestions at the end of the chapter on anger.

18

Sex as Rebellion

Have you ever noticed that telling children not to touch something makes them want to touch it all the more? Lift the ban and what happens? They lose interest. For whatever reasons, forbidding an activity makes it more desirable. This is particularly true when the activity is innately pleasurable and biologically driven, as is sex.

In our culture, legitimate sex is reserved for adulthood and is traditionally considered taboo until marriage. Thus sex has acquired an appeal beyond the simple function of satisfying a biological need. An individual might indulge in sex because it is forbidden, for the excitement to be found in the risk of getting caught, out of defiance, out of anger toward authority, or simply out of dissatisfaction with the existing social order. Sex arising from any of these motives is not only unsatisfying, but also creates a great deal of confusion in our relationships.

Those who indulge in sex purely out of defiance are in the minority. However, almost everyone's sex life has been affected to some degree by the fact that sex is a proscribed behavior. We shall discuss four ways in which this happens.

POST-CEREMONY LETDOWN

This phenomenon is familiar to many newly married couples who engaged in premarital sex. They report that sex after the ceremony is not nearly as exciting as it was before. Why is this so? During courtship many nonsexual needs are intertwined with the sexual aspect of the relationship, for example, confirmation of sexual identity, establishing of independence, rebellion, self-assertion, and mutual self-exploration. All of these needs are being satisfied—to some extent through sex, and to some extent through the evolving relationship.

Forming a new relationship is itself exciting and a source of considerable emotional satisfaction, but couples often mistakenly attribute the satisfaction to sex alone. After the ceremony these nonsexual needs are satisfied outside of the bedroom. For example, the need for independence is satisfied by establishing a new household, separate from parents. The need for rebellion or self-assertion is satisfied by forming values, establishing personal rules, and developing new life styles. The satisfaction derived from meeting these nonsexual needs is now separate from sexual satisfaction.

The net effect *seems* to be a decrease in sexual pleasure. In essence, before the ceremony the pleasure and satisfaction derived from various nonsexual sources was attributed to sex alone. After the ceremony only the satisfaction and pleasure derived *from sex* is attributed to sex. Thus sex *seems* less exciting or meaningful.

This post-ceremony letdown is generally experienced by couples who are not introspective, who are not aware of their needs, feelings, and the consequences of their behavior. If they were, all these needs would have been parcelled out and understood prior to the ceremony; there would have been no confusing letdown afterwards.

Most couples make it through the post-ceremony letdown without serious problems. However, some do experience doubts about sex, indulge less frequently, and worry if sex will ever be the same. In most cases, however, the effect is temporary, and the majority of sexual relationships improve with experience.

CONTINUING A BAD RELATIONSHIP

Thousands of couples continue relationships they would dissolve if sex were not a forbidden activity. There are two ways in which this happens:

Equating Love with Sex
Many couples believe that sex is wrong if they are not married or in love. Some of these couples delude themselves into believing they are in love to justify their having sex. After the novelty of sex wears off, the absence of love and the couples incompatibility become obvious. Guilt emerges, and they have two choices: face the guilt and break off the relationship, or continue the relationship under the guise of love on the grounds that "We have too much invested in each other to quit now."

Many couples who confess that "I felt from day one we never should have been married" most likely were caught in such a trap. These victims equate sex with love, as the following case illustrates.

Geraldine came for individual therapy because her fourth "serious" relationship in the last year was on the rocks. In each relationship she felt she was deeply in love and wanted to marry her boyfriend. She clung to each partner and was positive that her love was reciprocated. When asked how she could be so positive her reply was, "What do you mean how did I know he loved me? He had sex with me, didn't he!"

Geraldine had been raised by religious parents to believe that premarital sex was a serious sin unless a couple was in love and planned to get married. In her eyes, only a common whore had sex with "boyfriends." As therapy progressed, Geraldine came to realize that falling in love so easily was an excuse to have sex. She convinced herself that she was in love in order to get around her parents' unreasonable, puritanical standards. Her sexual relationships were a way of defying her tyrannical, overzealous parents. Geraldine's therapy consisted of developing her own set of values and sexual ethics.

Partners in Rebellion

Establishing a personal code of ethics requires considerable thought and independence of judgment. Some individuals never manage this; they never learn to think for themselves.

Instead, they depend on peers for support and encouragement as they flounder around searching for guidance. In many cases the supportive peer is an assertive individual of the opposite sex who is also rebelling and searching. When sex enters the relationship, a hidden partnership—an alliance between two rebels—forms.

Sex in such a relationship is used to confirm that neither party accepts traditional standards. It becomes the symbol of their independence and their break from old-fashioned restrictions. Problems develop if the partners do not help each other develop and solidify a new personal identity and code of ethics. Once sexual novelty wears off, and sex loses its symbolic meaning, the alliance outlives its function.

At this stage, the rebellion against authority becomes focused against each other. The mental and physical energies previously spent attacking the old-fashioned values are now used to attack one another. The couple's relationship deteriorates to one of mutual knitpicking and fault-finding, as the following case illustrates.

Martha was a 22-year-old statistician who came for therapy because she was thoroughly unhappy. She and her boyfriend had an extremely stormy relationship. He said he wanted to marry her. She was tempted to give in but she also felt it would be downright foolish since they could not get along now.

Martha was convinced that they loved each other, so she couldn't understand why they did not get along. To her, the fact that they always came back to one another was proof of their love. (In truth, it was proof of their hidden dependency.)

When Martha was encouraged to examine their relationship more closely, she could find nothing of value, no mutual caring, and few examples of loving behavior. Bill mistreated her frequently, yet she felt she could not leave him. Martha described him as a cool individual, who knew "where it was at," how to think for himself and get what he wanted.

A case history revealed that Martha had met him as she entered college. He literally swept her into bed with his indepedent and defiant attitude. Martha said, "I guess I liked the way he was able to see through things and didn't accept anything just because an expert said so. . . . He can give a critical analysis of anything and anybody." Unfortunately, after the novelty of sex wore off, he turned his critical powers on her. From then on their relationship was pure hell. Martha could not give Bill up, in spite of encouragement from her friends who saw him as an intelligent but immature jerk.

In therapy Martha came to realize that she was dependent on Bill, not in love with him. She had originally wanted to become independent of "her backward family." Yet Martha never developed her own values. She met Bill when she was just beginning to establish her own identity; instead of continuing to use her own resources, she let him take over. She came to depend on him to think for her.

To give up Bill, she would have to begin with the "backward values" of her family and develop her own code of ethics. This was a frightening prospect for Martha, but through therapy she gained the courage to do it.

These cases make three important points:

First, stormy relationships with frequent splitting up and reconciliation usually indicate a hidden mutual dependency. Repeated reconciliations usually have little to do with love.

The couple simply cannot let go of what both know is a terrible relationship.

Second, everyone must develop a personal code of sexual ethics. We have two choices in life. We can either accept completely what we have been taught about sex, or we can carefully analyze and evaluate what we have been taught and develop our own standards. Whatever our choice, we must live by the code we adopt or pay the price in our personal relationships.

Third, a rebellious individual cannot tolerate restrictions or limitations. All relationships have inherent restrictions because each partner becomes committed to the welfare of the other. Each surrenders some individual freedoms for the couple's common good. When rebels form relationships, these restrictions eventually become the target of their rebelliousness. Their partners become symbols of parental or social authority that must be conquered and subjugated. Knitpicking and faultfinding in such relationships are simply side issues. The rebels must attack and demolish their partners, the new symbol of old authority.

In short, rebels cannot form egalitarian relationships. Driven to fight and conquer ghosts from their past, they make their partners the victims. The only cure is for the rebel to establish, cherish, and live by a personal code of ethics. There is nothing to rebel against in a self-developed code for living.

Individuals who have sex out of rebelliousness neither accept parental morals nor establish a new personal code. They are doomed to a sex life dictated by their defiance of an old-fashioned ethic. (This differs from sex out of guilt, in which the individual accepts the old standards but cannot live up to them.)

ADOLESCENT TURMOIL

Adolescents are particularly susceptible to nonsexual sex. The illicit or forbidden aspect of sex appeals to them for many reasons. Indulging in sex: (a) can conveniently be used as a way of defying authority; (b) can be used to prove man or womanhood; (c) is a way of asserting one's self, defining personal values as opposed to accepting parental dictates; (d) is a way for adolescents to align themselves with their peers; (e) may be a way of confirming that the existing social expectations are unrealistic and valueless.

In effect, sex can and does appeal to adolescents for any of the nonsexual reasons discussed in this book. The entanglement of these motives, coupled with the search for identity and the emerging biological aspects of sex, makes adolescents particularly vulnerable to having sex for reasons other than sexual enjoyment. The fact that sex is off limits to them creates yet another nonsexual motive to drive their sexual behavior.

THE PERPETUAL ADOLESCENT

Many adolescents simply have sex out of the pleasure of doing something bad or forbidden. Some continue this defiance well into adulthood, becoming involved in unconventional sex, swinging, group sex, or extramarital affairs. This need to indulge in the forbidden can also lead to a number of destructive relationships as the following case illustrates.

Paul was a succesful attorney who had been married for six years. He considered his marriage very good and was pleased with his three children. Despite the seemingly ideal situation, his married life had been punctuated with several affairs. Some of the women, by his own account, did not even appeal to him. He simply took them to bed.

His ploys had begun in early adolescence and included one of his teachers, his minister's wife, and a close relative. Paul could find no rhyme or reason for his behavior. He came for therapy after seducing his wife's sister. When Paul finished listing his escapades, the following exchange took place.

Therapist. That's quite an impressive list.

Paul (beaming) I guess so!

Therapist. (chiding) You must have a set of brass balls.

Paul. (surprised) Huh!?

Therapist. Going after some of those women. You must be down-right brazen and determined.

Paul. (smiling) Oh, yeah! That's right! I am! (with emphasis and pride) It helps in the business I'm in.

Therapist. How's that?

Paul. I take cases no one wants. The ones my partner thinks we should refuse. They can't be won, or won big. I show 'em how to get milk from a stone. Or they'll tell me not to use a certain tactic because it might backfire and turn the court against me. (relates example)

Therapist. So you take the impossible and succeed. How do you decide which cases you'll take or which tactic you'll use?

Paul. Well, it seems that if my partner's against it, I'm for it. Someone else says no, I say go. Sounds kind of unprofessional and illogical, I guess.

Therapist. Do you see any connection between this and your exploits with women.

Paul. God, no! I keep my sex life separate from my career. Besides, I see a woman I want and I go after her, simple as that.

Therapist. Yes, but how do you decide which ones you want? By your own admission, some of them don't appeal to you in any way. (tauntingly) Must be that you're hard up and you'll take anybody that's willing.

Paul. (obviously angry but trying to smile) Hell no! I'm good at what I do. I get the ones *I* want. I've had women everyone knew were hands-off property. (leaning forward and pointing) You show me a woman you think I can't get and I'll show you! (threatening and loud) Nobody tells me who I can and can't sleep with. Nobody tells me what to do. Do ya hear! Nobod . . . (Paul falls back in his chair, looking embarrassed and sullen. He remains silent for about two minutes, then looks up.) I guess the prosecution rests its case.

Therapist. I'm not your prosecutor, but I have a feeling you've been fighting one all your life. Who are you fighting?

Paul went on to realize that his sex life was a rebellion in disguise. His real fight was with his father, who had placed one restriction and obstacle after another in the way of Paul's attempts to become successful and independent.

Paul's case is important because it demonstrates sex motivated entirely by rebellion as well as the cure for such behavior. These individuals must emotionally face the person they are rebelling against—usually an authority figure from the past, often but not always a parent.

What happens to old rebels? Those who do not face the real issues are likely to follow one of two courses. For some, the battle loses its joy; sex becomes less pleasurable. They attribute this decrease in pleasure to the ravages of time, instead of to the price of war. Others undergo religious conversion and sex fades into the background. Unfortunately, these converts become authoritarian and repeat the same pattern with their offspring. Thus the cycle is complete and self-perpetuating, passed from one generation to the next.

Why do we continue to proscribe, forbid, and rail against sex? Common sense as well as history tells us that these tactics do not work. They never did. They never will. (Remember Prohibition?) Organized religion has tried to wipe out pre and extramarital sex for centuries. In some cultures the offenders were put to death, yet sex continued unabated. Like it or not, we cannot legislate morality. The forbidden behavior simply goes underground and we merely become less aware of how our lives are influenced by this hidden motive, the desire to rebel.

* * *

The best way to prevent this misuse of sex is to teach self-awareness and self-respect and to make ourselves aware of the nonsexual ways in which we use sex, something we must all do for ourselves. (The exercises at the end of the chapters on social pressure and guilt apply here.) People who do not formulate their own standards will continue to rebel against others and will remain ignorant of their own wants and needs.

"OF COURSE I KNOW MY BOYFRIENDS INTIMATELY. JOE LIKES IT MISSIONARY STYLE WEARING BLACK SOCKS. PAUL WANTS REAR ENTRY AND TO HOWL LIKE A COYOTE. JACK LIKES IT IN THE GARAGE....."

PART II

UNDERSTANDING NONSEXUAL SEX

19

How It Happens

How is it that sex, a simple, pleasurable activity, becomes entangled with so many nonsexual needs and motives? Over time we *learn* to misuse sex—through two basic processes: (1) conditioning, and (2) modeling and learned attitudes.

CONDITIONING

Conditioning, the most basic type of learning, is the repeated pairing of two objects, ideas, feelings, or behaviors until the occurrence of one recalls the other.

For example, every time Aunt Molly visits, she gives Bobbie a present. Bobbie learns to associate Aunt Molly with the good feeling of getting a present. It is really the present that stimulates the good feelings, but in Bobbie's mind it is Aunt Molly. Thus, Bobbie learns to see Aunt Molly as the cause of her good feelings. But Bobbie also learns to expect a gift every time she sees Aunt Molly.

Suppose Aunt Molly stops the gift giving. What happens? Bobbie feels disappointed. Aunt Molly's visits are not as much fun as they used to be! If gift giving were the only bond between

Bobbie and Aunt Molly, and the number of gifts decreased, Bobbie would lose interest and poor Aunt Molly would be out in the cold.

In a similar way, sex becomes conditioned to or associated with nonsexual needs. The ways this can happen are (1) visual and fantasy conditioning, (2) verbal conditioning, (3) *in vivo* conditioning, and (4) conditioning through modeling and learned attitudes.

Visual and Fantasy Conditioning

Let's see how sex becomes intertwined with boredom through visual and fantasy conditioning. Johnny, age 16, feels bored. He cannot think of anything to do. He becomes listless and wanders around the house, discovers some hidden issues of *Playboy*, and takes them to his room. As he leafs through, admiring and enjoying the photos, his imagination takes over. He no longer feels bored. He is aroused, and nature takes its course.

In this case, sex has alleviated boredom. Next time Johnny feels bored, guess what he is going to do. You bet! And guess what Johnny is learning—to use sex to deal with boredom. If he repeats this pattern often, as a married adult he will seek sex from his wife whenever he is bored.

This behavior pattern has serious repercussions. Sex cannot completely satisfy nonsexual needs, boredom in Johnny's case. Johnny will consequently feel dissatisfied and blame "poor sex." Just as Bobbie lost some enthusiasm for Aunt Molly, Johnny will lose some enthusiasm for sex. No one maintains high interest in anything that proves unsatisfying or frustrating.

One more example, this time considering anger. Johnny has just had a rift with his parents; instead of feeling bored, he is angry. He storms off to his room, sulks, pouts, and sputters. Eventually he picks up the magazines and begins to look at them. His anger subsides and sexual feelings surface. He is learning to use sex to deal with anger.

In a similar manner, Johnny can learn to use sex to deal with any emotion or problem. If he feels sad and resorts to *Playboy*, he is using sex to ward off depression. If he feels lonely or down on himself and resorts to sexual fantasy to make himself feel good, he is again teaching himself to misuse sex. In all instances, sexual, visual stimuli and fantasy are paired with some feeling state. Repeated pairings condition the misuse of sex.

Verbal Conditioning

Conditioning can also take place on a verbal level. Instead of bringing gifts on each visit, Aunt Molly may simply make pleasing remarks to Bobbie, such as, "My, you look spiffy in that outfit." The same conditioning will take place. The resultant good feelings from the compliment become paired with Aunt Molly.

How can this apply to sex? Easily. Just think of the many emotions we pair with sexual words or phrases. Here are just a few examples:

Anger:	That bitch can suck my dick! That bastard can kiss my ass!
Affection:	Mmm, I'd like to snuggle between her boobs. Yeah, I'd like to squeeze his buns.
Humiliation:	Man, I'd eat her shit just to get near enough to kiss her ass. (self-humiliation) I'd like to tear her clothes off and let everybody see what she's got. He's such a nerd in bed he can't find his own thing—what there is of it.
Revenge:	I'd like to shove my cock in her stuck up face! She can lick the sweat off my balls. (because she cheated on him) If he flirts with one more of my friends, I'll

shove his head under her skirt and smother him to death.

Loneliness:
I don't care what he's after. I gotta have a date. It's better than staying home.
Kiss her a few times. She's hard up.

Avoiding intimacy:
Who cares! Put a bag over his (her) face! Upside-down they're all the same.
All men (women) are alike!
I'd go to bed with him if he promised not to open his mouth. His conversation is the pits.

Sexual identity:
I'd show her (him) what a good lover is! They don't know what good sex is until they get me!
I'd go to bed with him (her) just to say that I had.

Security:
Show him (her) a good time and he (she) won't want to go out with anyone else.

What is so bad about making these comments? In and of themselves, nothing. However, repeated usage encourages us to see sex as a vehicle for revenge, humiliation, coping with loneliness, and so on. Each time we pair nonsexual emotions with sexual images we are preparing the way for misusing sex.

In Vivo Conditioning

In vivo is a $2.00 phrase which means "in life," "in actuality" or "in reality." This type of sexual conditioning usually occurs within a relationship. Each partner conditions the other to use sex to satisfy hidden nonsexual motives.

One example will suffice. Herb comes home from the factory looking worn and unhappy. Sharon, his wife, becomes solicitous and affectionate. They end up in bed. Afterwards Herb feels better, and has learned that sex makes his depression subside. Sharon has learned that she can make Herb's sadness go away with a treat in bed. By repeating this sequence they condition each other to use sex to alleviate depression. More examples of couples conditioning each other to engage in nonsexual sex are found throughout this book.

Modeling and Learned Attitudes

Finally, we learn to misuse sex through the attitudes modeled by significant people in our environment—parents, peers —and by advertising and film media. We will consider parental influence first.

Parental attitudes are probably the most potent factors shaping our feelings and beliefs about sexual matters. Parents convey their attitudes both by what they say and by what they do not say about sex. For example, if parents discuss sex openly and in positive terms, they convey a healthy attitude to their children. On the other hand, if they never discuss sex, their children get the idea that there is something wrong with it. Children are greatly influenced by what they see and hear in the home. Consider these examples.

If mom and dad never kiss each other except in the bedroom the kids learn to see sex as the primary source of affection. If mom and dad soothe each other's ruffled feelings with pillow talk, the kids learn to see sex and anger as bedfellows. If parents preach against sex as disgusting or sinful, the kids learn to see sex as a vehicle for humiliation.

Parents convey sexual attitudes in many ways. Consider the possible associations children can learn when one parent pats the other's behind. If the recipient smiles, a healthy, "sex is fun" attitude is conveyed. If the reaction is annoyance, sex and anger are paired. If the recipient responds with a kiss, sex and affection are bonded. An embarrassed response pairs sex with humiliation.

In essence, the attitudes modeled by our parents predisposed us to see and use sex as they did. But consider these three points:

1. It is the repeated display of a particular attitude that

exerts a strong influence on the child. One pairing or display is insignificant.

2. Children do not automatically adopt parental attitudes *in toto*. There is usually some natural, personal modification between generations.

3. You do not have to fit the mold cast by your parents. Their examples and attitudes make it much easier for you to misuse sex just as they did. However, you can avoid the trap by becoming aware of how *their* attitudes influence *your* sex life.

Peers also help to shape our attitude toward sex and influence our sexual behavior. Adolescents are particularly susceptible to the influence of what others think, say, and do. During these pre-adult years they have many needs that make them vulnerable to many popular misconceptions or abuses of sexuality. Primarily, they need to belong, to feel socially accepted and popular, to feel important and to know that they make a difference. Adolescents also need to break parental ties, discover their own values and meaning in life, and to deal with their emerging sexuality.

Thus, how their peers talk about sex and what they say about those who have sex exerts a powerful influence on their own sexual behavior. Teens who cannot clearly delineate between sexual and nonsexual needs are at a distinct disadvantage. They will confuse the two and become the sexual victims of their nonsexual needs. They will have sex when they really want and need something else:

- to increase their popularity.
- to prove they are desirable, masculine, or feminine.
- to talk to and be with an understanding friend.
- to get a date or to have something to do.
- to rebel against parental authority.

In short, adolescents can be victimized by all of the nonsexual needs listed in the previous chapters. Their bodies, minds, and personalities are in a state of flux. They are more vulnerable than adults, lacking the integration that comes with age and maturity. They are apt to imitate their peers regarding sexual matters rather than think for themselves. It is our responsibility to make them aware of the possible misuses of sex.

Television and movies also train us to associate nonsexual needs with sex. Soap operas, for example, flagrantly show couples having sex out of desperation or loneliness, to gain affection, for revenge, and for many other nonsexual reasons. We constantly witness people bedding together in order to kill, obtain secret information, or blackmail. Sex for the sake of sex is seldom seen.

Television and magazine advertisements bombard us with innuendos that associate sex appeal with everything from drinking beer to replacing a muffler. We subconsciously relate sex to the feelings associated with the product. In this way we increase our chances for misusing sex.

Finally, television, and movies are guilty of promoting sex-role stereotypes. As was mentioned earlier, maintaining such stereotypes hampers our ability to enjoy sex freely and spontaneously. We end up making love to an idea instead of a person.

In summary we have all learned certain attitudes toward sex that predispose us to misuse it in any number of ways. To fully explore and enjoy sex we must first examine these sexual attitudes and beliefs. We must also consider how others have influenced our sexual behavior and continue to do so. Finally we must determine how we may be perpetuating these maladaptive sexual patterns.

20

Why It Continues

In the previous chapter we saw how people learn to misuse sex through conditioning and modeling. Behavioral psychologists believe that for conditioning to remain effective there must be occasional, at least partial, reinforcement. For example, if an individual is using sex to alleviate anger, the sex must at least partially alleviate the anger or the two will not remain associated.

Sex *does* give partial satisfaction to nonsexual motives. In fact, partial satisfaction of the nonsexual need serves as the reinforcement that perpetuates the misuse of sex. How does this happen? Certain sexual behaviors can satisfy sexual as well as nonsexual needs. For example, kissing can be affectionate or sexual; biting can satisfy angry or sexual impulses. Let us take a closer look at how this happens.

UNFINISHED BUSINESS

Unfinished business refers to feelings and needs that have been repressed because they were not expressed or satisfied at the time they were experienced. According to Gestalt psychologists, these feelings do not dissipate; they remain in our psyche, waiting for an opportunity to surface and find expression.

Attempting to find resolution, these unexpressed feelings distort our perceptions and color our interactions. In effect, they seep out when our guard is down, in situations that resemble the one in which they were originally created. The greater the pressure from the unfinished business, the greater the likelihood that it will come out in an inappropriate situation. No doubt you have heard the expression "an accident looking for a place to happen." Well, that is unfinished business, a feeling (anger) looking for an excuse to be expressed (explode).

To illustrate, consider a man with a short fuse. He has a lot of repressed anger that was not expressed when or toward whom it was first felt. This repressed anger creates internal pressure. It wants out. As the pressure builds, his perceptions become more distorted. He sees threat where none exists and he lashes out. He feels attacked when friendliness is intended and lashes out. He feels angry when help is offered and again lashes out. In short, he finds, even creates, reasons to explode and get rid of some of that repressed anger.

Others are apt to see him as an unstable grouch, a chronic complainer, oversensitive, or a downright ornery cuss. Following his release of anger he becomes a relatively calm, nice guy. But most people will keep their distance and avoid prolonged or intimate contact. They simply find him too unpredictable and do not want to be the butt of his unprovoked anger.

In fact, he suffers from the effects of repressed anger (unfinished business). If he could resolve this anger, he would become a normal, fairly even-tempered individual. He would experience more satisfying interpersonal relationships.

In the case of the man with the short fuse, his repressed anger may seek expression in furious and excessive pumping, biting, squeezing or other acts which are at odds with the natural flow of the developing sexual rhythm. His behavior will be perceived as inconsiderate and he will become known as a rough, extremely passionate lover.

Unfortunately his intensity stems from the need to express anger, not sexuality. Camouflaging anger in the sexual act will not satisfy this need. It will surface again and again, perpetuating his reputation as a rough or inconsiderate lover. If he could resolve the repressed anger, his sex life would improve; he would be free to focus on his sexual impulses, uncontaminated by hidden anger. His behavior in bed would syncronize with the sexual energy and tension which develops as the act proceeds. Any furious pumping would stem from intense sexual feelings and impulses arising from the mutual passion of receptive lovers.

And so it is with any unfinished business—the need for affection, the need to feel important, competent, in control or worthy—each can and will seep into the bedroom and rob lovers of pleasure. Any sexual behavior arising from these needs will be out of syncronization, inappropriate to the level of tension and sexual energy building between the partners. If the unfinished business continues to surface in the bedroom, problems develop and the couple comes to see themselves as sexually incompatible.

Take the case of Linda, a housewife who felt unimportant and incompetent. To compensate for her feelings of inadequacy, she became skillful in the bedroom. She was always very intense and passionate—carried away by what seemed to be uncontrolable sexual impulses. Initially both she and her husband, Mark, enjoyed her performance. However, there were times when Mark wanted tender, quiet sex. Linda's zeal seemed out of place and overrode any attempt he made to keep it gentle and romantic. Linda perceived Mark's attempts at tenderness as a rejection of her sexuality. The pressure to be the best caused her to redouble her efforts, which frustrated Mark even more. Neither felt satisfied after these experiences, which increased in frequency.

Eventually they learned to see themselves as sexually incompatible and decided to seek professional help. In therapy

Linda learned how to feel competent outside the bedroom, and Mark learned to express his needs more directly and openly in the bedroom.

There are three things to keep in mind about unfinished business. First, everyone experiences it. No one can express all of his/her feelings as they arise. Second, the more unfinished business we carry around, the more pressure it exerts, and the better the chances it will surface in inappropriate ways. Third, unfinished business will seek resolution any time and any place. The bedroom is no exception. In fact, the bedroom is ideal! Why?

Sexual behavior is a very complex chain of acts that culminates in intercourse. The links of the chain consist of independent acts, such as kissing, touching, squeezing, and pumping. These acts are already associated with sex as well as with many nonsexual feelings, needs, or motives (See the table on page 158). For example, the love squeeze or bite can be associated with sex, aggression, revenge, anger, resentment, or hunger; so any unfinished business related to these needs can easily surface at this time. You may, if you have considerable unexpressed anger, get carried away with the biting or squeezing and cause pain or physical harm to your partner.

Hector's is a case in point. A sincere family man, he boasted that he never argued with his wife despite their strong personal differences, and some of her habits that annoyed him. She expressed her needs, and Hector, "like a true gentleman," always deferred. In bed he was very aggressive. According to his wife, his lovemaking became excessively passionate. One night he got carried away with his squeezing, biting, and love pats and literally slapped her silly.

This, of course, is an extreme example. In most cases the nonsexual does not surface so blatantly. It is usually subtle and remains outside the individual's awareness. Throughout sex there will be a mild conflict, wherein the sexual and non-sexual needs compete for satisfaction and resolution. Consequently, neither need is completely satisfied. The result is a frustrated or letdown feeling after sex, a feeling that, even though the mechanics of sex went well, something was missing. Martha G's case illustrates the problem well.

Martha's boss was highly critical of a financial presentation she gave to the Board. She felt the criticism was excessive, and was angry, but she could not express her anger to her boss in any meaningful or satisfying manner. She swallowed her pride and tried to forget about it.

Her next sexual experience proved to be very unsatisfying. Her partner was good and Martha was very active—"more so than usual." Thus, she was at a loss to explain why she felt frustrated afterward. "I felt like I was holding back. Just couldn't let go." Her partner was also confused. He thought Martha had shown an excellent combination of aggression and passivity.

In fact, Martha's unfinished business had seeped into her sex life. Her angry feelings and her sexual needs were competing for satisfaction. Neither was completely satisfied. Martha thought that she was *sexually* frustrated, that she was holding back *sexual* impulses, because she was only aware of her sexual needs. In truth, she was holding back aggressive nonsexual impulses. Her body knew that she was having sex and wanted to focus on that, but her unfinished business was putting out competing impulses. Her body was torn between striking out in anger and having sex. She had to keep a very tight lid on the anger to complete the sex act. Is it really surprising that sex was less enjoyable?

In summary, it is our early conditioning experiences that teach us to use sex to satisfy nonsexual needs. It is unfinished business, surfacing during sex, that perpetuates this cycle. Sex is always less pleasureable when our body and mind try to focus on and satisfy the two competing needs simultaneously.

Any or all of the behaviors mentioned in Table I can be used to please ourselves, our partners or both. And in each case the motive behind the behavior can be sexual or nonsexual; any sexual behavior can arise from any number of motives or needs.

Keep in mind, first, that the same behavior, such as kissing or licking, can have many different meanings. Licking an armpit can mean something completely different from licking earlobes, lips, or an anus, while licking toes can have still another meaning.

Second, a given behavior, in and of itself, does not automatically have nonsexual significance. The behaviors listed above can stimulate or satisfy both sexual or nonsexual needs. Usually, nonsexual needs fade into insignificance and remain in the background during sex. It is when the nonsexual needs become part of the foreground that they detract from sexual satisfaction.

There are several reasons why sex allows such a wide range of emotional needs to surface. First, it is basically a nonthinking activity; we generally do not think about or analyze what we are doing. Second, in the heat of passion our inhibitions are relaxed and our bodies take over. It is easy for unfinished business to break through because our guard is down. The third reason—the clincher—is that the component parts of sex are easily, if not already, associated with nonsexual needs, as illustrated in Table I. All in all, the sex act is an ideal time for all kinds of repressed feelings, motives, and needs to surface and seek satisfaction.

In fact, all of us are peripherally aware of the possible nonsexual motives of sexual behavior. We label our lovers according to acts they favor. A lover who touches gently and kisses a great deal is called an affectionate lover; one who pumps long and hard is passionate; another, who touches roughly and squeezes hard, may be called aggressive. We seldom consider that they may have nonsexual reasons for their preferences. For example, the rough lover may be an angry, hostile person.

TABLE I

NONSEXUAL NEEDS WHICH CAN BE LINKED TO SEXUAL BEHAVIOR

Behavior	Motives, Needs, and Desires Which Can Be Linked to the Behavior

Touching	We can touch:
	    gently out of affection or to reassure.
	    timidly because we need reassurance.
	    roughly because we are angry.
	    boldly to prove dominance.
	    violently to instill fear or subjugate.

Kissing	We can kiss:
	    to demonstrate love or respect.
	    to soothe hurt feelings.
	    to appease anger.
	    to reassure.
	    to express affection or intimacy.
	    to hide loneliness and fear.
	    to stimulate passion.
	A kiss also can be patronizing, such as a kiss on the forehead accompanied by a pat on the head, or humiliating as when someone kisses you when or where you do not want to be kissed.

Undressing	We can make ourselves naked:
	    to embarrass or humiliate someone.
	    to force someone to see what he or she would prefer not to.
	    to assert ourselves.
	    to seek praise and reassurance.
	We can strip someone naked:
	    out of sexual passion.
	    to have sex.
	    out of anger.
	    out of defiance.
	    to hurt or humiliate.
	    out of fear.
	    to subjugate.

TABLE I (Continued)

Caressing Massaging Squeezing	We can indulge in these behaviors: 　　to be helpful and please our partner. 　　to cause pain. 　　to feel in control and powerful. 　　to cling in desperation. We can submit to our partner's touch: 　　out of loneliness or subservience. 　　because we feel helpless or abused. 　　to enjoy.
Penetration	We can penetrate: 　　to explore. 　　to give pleasure. 　　to be close and intimate. 　　to subjugate or dominate. 　　to humiliate or violate. 　　to inflict pain. 　　in anger. 　　to verify sexuality.
Pumping	We can pump: 　　intensely from sexual passion. 　　violently from anger or hate. 　　timidly from fear. 　　in joy or ecstasy. 　　desperately from a need to cling. 　　wildly to lose control. 　　submissively to be dominated or to escape 　　　　into oblivion.

The affectionate lover may be a dependent or affection-starved individual.

Of course, not everyone with a strong preference for certain behaviors during sex is having nonsexual sex. However, if there is an excessively strong preference and sex is not satisfying, nonsexual motives are certainly at work.

The point is that during sex there is ample opportunity for the nonsexual to surface. A lover who cannot or does not express emotions openly outside the bedroom will have many chances to express the emotion indirectly during sex. These indirect expressions are never really satisfying. The relief afforded through sex is minimal and the need will resurface again and again, each time taking its toll on sexual pleasure.

Thus the question is not "Is it possible to misuse sex?" but, rather, "Is it possible to not misuse sex?" The answer is yes, it is possible. But it requires thoughtful awareness—awareness of *all* our needs, sexual and nonsexual. We must make sure that the nonsexual needs are satisfied outside the bedroom, so that during sex they will recede into insignificance. Only then can the sexual surface full force. Only then can we reap our full measure of sexual pleasure and satisfaction.

21

The Dangers of Nonsexual Sex

Right now you might be thinking, "What's really so bad about having sex for hidden, nonsexual reasons? Maybe my sex life isn't *all* that it could be, but so what?"

If diminished pleasure were the only problem, your point might be well taken. However, nonsexual sex creates additional problems that affect the individual, the couple, their relationship *and* their sex life. First, consider three important ways in which sex itself is affected by nonsexual motives: (1) sexual pleasure and satisfaction are decreased; (2) interest in sex diminishes; (3) sexual maturity is inhibited.

DECREASED PLEASURE AND SATISFACTION

The body and mind cannot focus on and satisfy two unrelated needs. When sex is used to satisfy any nonsexual emotional need, a reduction in physical pleasure and satisfaction is inevitable. Unfortunately, sex will bear the brunt of this dissatisfaction because we are not aware of the other needs. We are apt to question our sexual technique and prowess, or those of our partner.

As stated before, we must learn to look outside the bedroom for the real cause. Blaming ourselves or our partners only adds more anxiety to sex and reduces sexual pleasure even further. No one can fully enjoy sex amid doubts of sexual adequacy.

DIMINISHED SEXUAL INTEREST

When nonsexual motives influence our sex lives, interest in sex decreases on both the short- and long-term levels. First consider the immediate effect. One of the basic tenets of behavioral science is that the more pleasure an act produces, the more inclined we are to repeat the act when the opportunity arises; the less pleasurable an act, the less likely we are to repeat it. Thus, when hidden motives detract from sexual pleasure we will be less inclined to take advantage of the next opportunity to have sex. (This does not mean that the human species is in any danger of extinction.)

Of course, even when used for nonsexual purposes, sex gives some pleasure. It is not likely that we will give it up completely after a few mediocre experiences. But there will be a definite decrease in sexual interest. It is natural to become less interested in activities that do not produce their expected pleasure or satisfaction. This short-term decrease in interest and enthusiasm often goes unnoticed. We usually have an ample armament of ready-made excuses—headache, backache, office work, not in the mood—and we tend to accept these excuses as the natural course of events, as temporary blocks to having sex.

We may become aware of our declining sexual enthusiasm only as the relationship ages and the excuses become more frequent. If we have courage we see the excuses for what they are: *rationalizations for a declining enthusiasm for sex.* If we continue to avoid the truth, we pass the decline off as advancing age ("What do you expect? We've been having sex for ten years. It's bound to get less exciting.").

This is when couples are likely to resort to a once a week or once a month routine, assuming that it is only natural for sex to become less enjoyable after the novelty wears off and the years add up. On the contrary, as we become more experienced and confident and less inhibited, sex should become more enjoyable, intense, exciting, and satisfying. Enthusiasm for sex should increase and continue well into the twilight years. So, to automatically attribute a sexual decline to the advancing age of a relationship is unacceptable. The decline is more likely to be the result of burdening sex with nonsexual motives. For when sex is free of nonsexual motives, enthusiasm remains high, as long as the physiological apparatus works.

"I JUST SPOKE TO MOTHER. SHE SAID YOU SHOULD BE SATISFIED WITH ONCE A WEEK."

Those who use sex to satisfy nonsexual needs never feel completely satisfied after sex. They think they cannot learn to satisfy themselves sexually, and eventually give up trying. In fact, they cannot satisfy nonsexual emotional needs with sex. They should stop trying—not to satisfy their sexual needs but stop trying to satisfy their emotional needs through sex.

Consider this "almost" client. He was 34 years old and wanted therapy because he was *sure* he had a very serious sexual problem. He had no idea what was wrong, but he knew that something had to be amiss because, "I can't keep up with my father." To his dumbfounded listeners he related the following incident.

"We were visiting my parents, both of whom are retired. After eating, my dad and I adjourned to the living room. My wife came in to serve after-dinner drinks. My dad made an admiring comment on the sexiness of my wife's dress and her generous butt. She laughed and teasingly said, 'Oh, listen to the old stud. I thought you'd be too old to notice things like that.'

"My dad smiled and said something like 'Oh, you'd be surprised. Don't let the gray feathers fool you about this old gander. I'm every bit as active as your young buckeroo.'

"Well, Marge and I just looked at each other and said, 'Yeah, I'll bet you are.' Next thing we're all betting $10.00 whether my old man has sex more often than me. Marge and I figure we're above the national average so how can we lose. With the money down, Marge tells my dad he'd better tell the truth because she'll check with Mom. 'I know she'll tell it like it is,' warned Marge. 'She doesn't have the old male ego to protect.'

"At this point I still figure it's a joke. Then my dad says, 'I'm not going to say a word. Let Celeste tell you.' He then yells into the kitchen, 'Celeste! How often do we have sex?'

"After a long pause she calls back, 'You want me to say it out loud? What kind of conversation is that, anyway?'

"My dad yells back, 'Say it, sweetheart. I'll explain later.'

"Comes the sheepish, barely audible reply: 'Well, last month it was 30 days, 30 times. (pause) *At least!*'

"Marge and I didn't mind losing ten apiece, but we just couldn't believe it. We told Mom so. She replied, 'Well, I guess we are pretty old, but you know your daddy is very (blush) good. Besides, at my age you have fun whenever you can. Who knows how long it'll last!' "

One fact must be faced. When *any* activity loses its pleasure and satisfaction, we indulge less frequently, and eventually give it up completely. Sex is no exception! We hasten this process when we allow nonsexual motives to creep into our sex lives.

INHIBITED SEXUAL MATURITY

Sexual maturity is another one of those vague terms that can mean just about anything, from "having a sexual apparatus that works" to "knowing how to use it like a pro." In fact, sexual maturity is not a state of being as much as it is an attitude or process—an unending state of becoming.

No one *is* sexually mature—only working toward becoming so. Sexual maturity is not something that happens when we grow pubic hair or get married. It is a life-long process requiring time, effort, energy, and, above all, thought and self-awareness. It implies a willingness to consider what we are doing in bed in terms of our needs, our personality, and our responses and feelings, as well as those of our partners.

More than this, it means a willingness to explore, set goals, expand horizons, and fully experience the infinity of sex. This means setting our own comfort zones, designing our own limits and frequency charts, and making our own judgments about each experience. It also means accepting responsibility for our own pleasure, and our own sexual growth and development.

Consider this: What was just said about sexual maturity is

what psychologists say constitutes maturity in other areas. For example, emotionally mature individuals are self-aware, take risks to explore themselves, make independent judgments, set goals to achieve their potentials, and so on. Achieving maturity intellectually, emotionally, or spiritually requires self-aware-ness, self-examination—-and risk-taking as well as thorough planning. We must explore and experience all facets of these areas to achieve maturity (our potential). Why should we not do likewise with our sexual nature? Why should sex be an exception?

In fact, sex should *not* be an exception; we should experience and explore it to the fullest. But we cannot, as long as there are nonsexual motives influencing our sexual behavior. The first step toward sexual maturity is to rid sex of nonsexual motives, which make human sexuality like an iceberg: one-tenth seen, explored, and partially enjoyed; nine-tenths un-tried, unexplored, and unenjoyed. As long as nonsexual needs prevent the truly sexual from rising to the surface, we never experience the full intensity and pleaures of our sexual nature.

EFFECTS ON THE COUPLE

Nonsexual sex affects couples in long-term relationships pri-marily by (1) preventing emotional growth, (2) preventing closeness and creating distance, (3) causing jealousy and re-sentment, and (4) preventing sexual exploration and growth.

Preventing Emotional Growth
Emotionally mature individuals can recognize and satisfy their needs. To achieve this level of maturity, individuals must, first, be aware of their needs; second, learn to express them openly; and third, learn to seek effective, satisfying resolutions.

Using sex to satisfy nonsexual needs short-circuits this growth process. The nonsexual emotional needs remain hidden and imbedded in the sexual behavior, and the couple re-enacts the same problem over and over again. They do not acquire mature coping skills for the emotional problems that have been shunted into the bedroom, and they do not experience the emotional growth to be gained by working through real issues together. Their relationship remains at an infantile level.

This does not mean there is no growth and maturation. Rather, such couples tend to develop lopsided relationships, becoming reasonably close and mature in some areas, while remaining distant, egocentric, and infantile in others. Many of the case histories in this book are examples of lopsided relationships.

Preventing Closeness and Creating Distance

Nonsexual sex prevents closeness in two ways. First, any shared pleasurable experience draws people together; the participants feel closer, more intimate. When ulterior or hidden motives invade these shared times, intimacy is avoided and pleasure is diminished. Consider business lunches where ulterior motives abound. How enjoyable are these experiences? Often, neither the food nor the company is appreciated. So it is with sex driven by nonsexual needs. An otherwise pleasurable experience loses much of its power to bond people together. One or both partners feel frustrated. The usual reaction is to repress and not talk about the letdown. A sense of isolation develops when these feelings and concerns are not shared: distance is created.

Second, dealing with real issues, needs, or conflicts—and finding mutually satisfying solutions—draws couples together. When sex is used for nonsexual reasons, the real issues, needs, and conflicts never surface, and so cannot be shared and resolved. Each partner deals with his or her unverbalized needs alone. As a couple the partners do not make solid emotional contact and each feels a little more isolated.

Causing Jealousy and Resentment

Jealousy, a common side effect of nonsexual sex, is most likely to surface when one partner has serious problems with hidden nonsexual needs while the other is relatively free of them. The troubled partner will enjoy sex less and become jealous of the other partner's pleasure. These couples often battle over who does more work and who should pleasure whom. Soon they have two problems: the jealousy that surfaces as a pseudo-sexual problem, and the still hidden emotional problem. Of course, it does not stop here.

Feelings of resentment will surface in the partner who is relatively free of nonsexual motives, especially when the troubled partner is experiencing negative motives such as anger or humiliation, or is avoiding intimacy. In these cases the healthier partner is most likely to feel used, abused, or inadequate.

Even when both partners have nonsexual sex, jealousy and resentment are apt to set in and create additional problems. No two people use sex in the same way for the same nonsexual reasons. When one partner enjoys sex, the other probably will not and vice versa; when one partner is satisfied, the other will feel used or abused. The only real solution is to work on the problem as a couple. (We shall discuss the importance of this in the chapter on therapy.)

Preventing Sexual Exploration and Growth

When nonsexual needs infiltrate the bedroom, sexual exploration is inhibited for two primary reasons:

1. The nonsexual needs that creep into the bedroom prevent sexual feelings, impulses, and needs from surfacing full force. The nonsexual needs drain attention and energy from the sexual ones. Thus, sexual impulses cannot blossom, diversify, and be explored to any meaningful extent.

When nonsexual sex persists, our sexual natures remain unexplored, underdeveloped, and unenjoyed. We never learn the true depth and breadth of the human sexual experience. We sell sex short and assume that those few who claim to reach ecstasy simply exaggerate their experiences.

2. Second, and most important, sexual exploration involves

risk. The more sexual satisfaction and pleasure you receive, the easier it is to take risks. Why? If failure is met when satisfaction is high it will not be a catastrophe. When sexual satisfaction is minimal, as in nonsexual sex, risking a little is like risking everything. Failure seems disastrous.

It might seem that the opposite would be true: With so little satisfaction, why not risk finding something better? Because it is only human nature to opt for security. Consider the wage earner who barely survives. His sole pleasures in life are the weekly case of beer and two weeks in Florida. He would not be willing to give up his little pleasures for one year and risk another job, even with the promise of a better future. The beer and the trip are certainties. The future is not.

"YOU WANT TO KNOW THE REAL ME? WHAT DO YOU CALL THIS?"

Just as people with little money will not take financial risks, couples with little sexual satisfaction avoid sexual risks. In their concern to preserve the little they have, they blow the issue out of proportion and imagine that everything would be lost if they failed at something new. Thus, the sexual side of their relationship remains unexplored. Enjoyment remains minimal.

In effect, nonsexual sex creates a pseudo-sexual relationship. The couple's sex life is based not on sex as a medium of pleasure and mutual exploration but on a neurotic need that directs their sexual behavior. They miss the pleasure boat—and each other! They never really get to know each others' true emotional and sexual needs.

EFFECTS ON THE INDIVIDUAL

Single individuals might be tempted to say, "Why should I worry about hidden motives and meanings of sex? I'm too busy having fun!" It may behoove these individuals to recall that all married people were once single; and to consider that it is precisely this attitude and this lack of awareness that create sexual problems in a future relationship. The majority of the population take sex for granted, never bothering to scrutinize their sex lives or their beliefs about sex. (Ironically, if ignorance is bliss, why are so many people dissatisfied with sex? Why are "How to" books on sex in such demand?)

Whether he/she is single or married, nonsexual sex has serious effects on the individual. The repercussions mirror the effects on the couple so they will only be summarized here.

Sexual Growth Is Short-Circuited
People cannot develop a full capacity for sexual enjoyment when nonsexual needs are driving sexual behavior. Feelings of sexual pleasure will not be fully appreciated and individuals will be reluctant to explore their sexual natures and risk growth.

Emotional Growth Is Stunted

Integrated individuals are aware of their emotional needs, accept them, and learn to satisfy them. Individuals who use sex to "satisfy" nonsexual needs never learn to openly accept, express, or resolve emotional needs. As a result, these needs cannot be integrated into the self-image. Self-alienation results, and individuals may literally remain strangers to themselves.

Nonsexual Sex Creates Distance

Nonsexual sex makes true emotional contact difficult, if not impossible. It creates a pseudo-relationship based on a neurotic need. It may also lead to forced marriages or may prolong a neurotic relationship that should be discontinued (see the chapter on rebellion and sex).

In sum, the repercussions of nonsexual sex reach far beyond the bedroom and can seriously affect all aspects of our relationships and emotional well-being. To continue to view sex as a simple, uncomplicated act of pleasure is foolhardy. If we take our sex life for granted and never give it thoughtful consideration, we neglect a key aspect of our natures. We rob ourselves of the opportunity to discover and reach our full sexual potential. We also miss a whole lot of fun.

PART III

DISCOVERING
SEXUAL SEX

22

Sexual Sex: What Is It Like?

What is sex like when nonsexual motives are barred from the bedroom? First, and foremost, it is better than most people ever thought possible. Sexual pleasure seems to increase a hundredfold. Think of the *best* sex you ever had! Your partner was perfect; you were great; the mood, setting, and timing were fantastic. Sexual sex is all this and more!

When you are having sexual sex, all energy and attention is directed toward the same goal: good feelings. There are no distracting conflicts or hidden needs to interfere with the process of letting sexual energy and impulses flow and find satisfaction. Your body and psyche are integrated. It happens the way nature intended, unencumbered by nonsexual baggage.

Sexual sex can be a joyful contradiction. You may feel free and in control, yet overwhelmed and out of control. The sense of freedom and control is there because you are free from nonsexual influences. You have sex when you want sex, not because you are sad, affection-starved, or bored.

You may also feel overwhelmed and out of control. In fact, you will be—once sex is initiated. You will feel swept away as

175

your sexual needs press on toward satisfaction—lost in a barrage of sexual feelings and impulses, each bringing more pleasure than the last. At each stage of the act you will feel that your body and mind have exceeded their natural and spiritual capacities; you will explode in a paroxysm of delight. Your body will contract and relax in uncontrollable spasms of pleasure. You will be certain that you have reached beyond yourself, beyond reality, to the end of the universe. Your body and mind will intertwine with your partner's, every muscle fiber and every nerve ending tingling and contracting with pleasure.

Yes, you may feel overwhelmed and out of control. But as your body contracts with less intensity, a sense of calm, a quiet joy, a delightful satisfaction will gradually replace the crescendo of spasms. As you and your lover collapse in each other's arms, each will know where the other has been. Both have shared the experience.

Sexual sex can never be dull. There is always another avenue, another nerve fiber, another muscle contraction, a new feeling, a new depth into which you can plunge. Each trip opens a different corner of the mind and body, adding new dimensions to the relationship. Your body has billions of brain cells and thousands of miles of nerve and muscle fibers, each waiting to be explored. This is what sexual sex is all about: exploring the infinite variety of your own internal experience. You are in control in that *you* decide if and when you want sex. Once the experience begins, you are out of control, swept away by the excitement and intensity of the act. You give vent to the purely sexual; you allow sexual impulses to surface and follow their natural ebb and flow.

When the experience is over, you lie there—in awe of sex, of yourself, of your partner. You feel a powerful sense of intimacy, unity, and peace that comes from having made contact with the depth of your being and that of another human. You feel as if you have transcended a limit, penetrated a barrier, gone beyond yourself by going deeper inside. You have touched parts of yourself and your partner you did not know existed.

You have visited your innermost self and found it comfortable, exciting, and joyous: You have discovered your sexual nature. Explore to your heart's content. No one can tell exactly what sexual sex will be like for you. Only *you* can know and experience your body and mind working together to achieve sexual satisfaction. The experience is different for each of us. But make no mistake about it; when you have sexual sex, you will have no doubts! You will know you have experienced sex at its finest, unshackled by nonsexual needs.

GETTING THERE

Can everyone achieve sexual sex? Yes, *everyone* can. However, do not be deceived. Clearing the nonsexual motives from your sex life requires time, effort, and courage—courage to face the nonsexual needs, effort and patience to work through and resolve these needs or issues.

Courage is called upon again once the nonsexual baggage is eradicated—many lovers are disconcerted by the forceful intensity sex acquires. They tend to be overwhelmed and a little frightened because they have never been completely enveloped in their sexuality. Despite initial anxiety, of course, the pure joy of the experience encourages most people to try again—and soon. Comments such as the following are typical:

"What an experience! I was stunned. I felt afraid, carried away. I didn't know what was happening. I had no idea sex could be so intense."

"I don't know what really happened. This feeling just kept getting bigger and bigger. Like I was swept away on a giant wave. That thing had me. I was helpless. I could only go along with it. I got a little scared, but it was utterly fantastic. I can't wait 'til it happens again."

"What was it like? A little crazy, a little fearful, a lot of excitement and intensity. There's really no way to describe it, just WOW!"

"I felt lost after my climax. Like I had to pull myself together. I'd give anything to have all my sex feel that good, that intense."

"You mean it will happen again!? I thought I was having a big breakthrough! Like I went through some kind of barrier and now I can have adult sex, or something like that."

"It was as if my partner was a human rocket and we were shooting through space. The more I felt his fire and passions, the faster everything whizzed by. I was worried if I'd ever get back to earth. I've never felt anything like it."

"There's no one word to describe it. It was strange, exciting, and weird. I felt we were plunging into this dark abyss, tumbling and pumping as we fell. It was terribly exciting and scary. Then I realized I was falling into myself, my own mind. I don't know how else to describe it."

Without exception these individuals and couples go on to enjoy different types of experiences while maintaining high levels of pleasure and satisfaction. There is a remarkable change in their attitudes and feelings about sex.

"I don't know what I was having in bed before, but it couldn't have been sex . . . There's no similarity between now and then. . . . "

"Before, maybe one out of every twenty times sex was a real fireworks and bell-ringer type. Now I'll bet it's more like eight or ten out of every twenty. My sex life is *so* different."

"It's different every time. One time it was like my whole body was a giant heart, pumping and exploding in rhythms of pleasure. Another time I felt like a giant cock pulsating like mad with all these fantastic sensations as I pumped the semen out. . . . It's just so unbelievable and fantastic. . . . "

"Neither one of us can really say what it's like for the other, yet I feel we know without saying. It's too good to be true. Sometimes

I have this weird feeling that if I describe it or tell anyone else, I'll lose it or it will go away. It's like having a secret I'm dying to share. Yet I can't share it because it's never the same."

"That's a good question. It always seems like the same fantastic feeling, but everything else is different, totally different. I don't know. I just feel I've been to a different place each time and yet there's a unity or common thread."

"I'm not afraid to have sex as often as I'd like. I used to hold back because I thought if I had it too often I'd get bored. Now I know I held back because I was bored. Forcing myself to have it less often was my way of making it *seem* more exciting."

In addition to better sex, there are other rewards for eliminating the nonsexual baggage from your sex life. The following are some of the more frequently reported side effects, along with supporting comments from couples who experienced them.

Improved Relationship

"At first I was sure you were wrong. I thought if we had lots of affection without sex, sex would become meaningless and lack depth. Since we've been more affectionate with each other outside of the bedroom, sex has gotten better. The best part is now we find each other to be more pleasant and loving outside of the bedroom. It's like a second honeymoon that's going on and on."

"Our entire relationship has changed. Our bickering has stopped. We are less angry. We're pleased, very pleased. And sex is so much better."

Growth and Discovery

"The sexual goodies alone were worth it. I'm even more pleased with *me*. I feel at peace with myself—like I love me for the first time. I don't have to prove anything to anybody, including myself, in bed or out of it."

"I'm different. She's different. Or maybe we just turned on to different parts of us we never knew existed. I guess we hid a lot in the bedroom. . . . "

"Believe it or not, the great sex is the least of the benefits for us. Since we stopped trying to avoid boredom with sex, we've become two new people. We've done so many new things and developed so many new interests we're strangers to our old friends. Funny thing, though, we have more time for sex, not less as we thought we might."

Greater Intimacy

"Now that we have real sex, or whatever you want to call it, we are much more intimate. I feel I got to know the real Jim. (laughs) Maybe that's why I call it real sex. He feels the same way. We can't believe what we've been missing in and out of bed."

"We resolve our problems quicker because we deal with the real issues. We don't rely on the bedroom to even out the scores. We just know each other so much more."

" . . . Yeah, sex is a whole lot better. But so are we. We're closer. We know each other. We talk before we get to the bedroom. That's the best part."

In sum, sexual sex is within everyone's reach—but it requires effort and the willingness to face and explore yourself, your partner, and each other's sexual and nonsexual needs. The price is your effort, your time, and the discarding of a worn and tired facade. The rewards you reap are many and well worth the price. As these quotes testify, infinitely better sex is just the beginning.

23

Exploring Your Sex Life

In this chapter you can take an active role in analyzing your own sexual and emotional behavior and attitudes. As you answer the questionnaires, be truthful and keep an open mind. The only thing you have to lose is a mediocre sex life. The questionnaires are intended as helpful guideposts, not as a definitive judgment on the quality of your sex life or as a substitute for therapy.

To maximize sexual growth we must separate sexual from nonsexual needs, and seek their satisfaction outside of the bedroom. The questions below will help you determine which of your major nonsexual needs are not being satisfied out of bed. Read each statement and respond with your first inclination, either Yes or No.

———(a) I often feel I am being cheated.

———(b) I usually feel others are not listening to me.

———(c) I find it difficult to cooperate and work with others.

———(d) I am comfortable sharing my feelings.

——(e) I receive a fair share of attention and recognition at work.

——(f) I tend to avoid forming friendships.

——(g) My feelings are easily hurt.

——(h) I express my anger when appropriate.

——(i) I receive ample attention from my friends.

——(j) I feel others cannot be trusted.

——(k) I feel left out when in a group.

——(l) I express and discuss my hurt feelings comfortably with my partner.

——(m) I can often enjoy being alone.

——(n) I feel it is best not to reveal some of my thoughts and desires to my partner.

——(o) I feel my self-respect fluctuating, depending on what kind of feedback I am receiving from others.

——(p) There are things I would like to say to people (past or present) but I never seem to get around to it.

——(q) I can admit when I am lonely.

——(r) I receive plenty of attention from my family.

——(s) I seek emotional or physical contact when lonely or bored.

——(t) I feel most comfortable when I am in control of a situation.

——(u) I subscribe to definite sexual stereotypes.

——(v) I know what makes me feel worthwhile.

——(w) Most of my interpersonal problems are my fault.

——(x) When I see someone who is sad my inclination is to try to cheer them up.

——(y) I often carry a grudge.

——(z) I must have my own way.

Consider your answers in terms of the following key. It will suggest which of your emotional needs are most likely seeping into your sex life.

1. "Yes" answers to items d, e, h, i, l, m, q, r, and v suggest that most of your nonsexual needs are presently being met.

2. "No" answers to the following items suggest that one or more of the accompanying nonsexual motives could be entering your sex life.

d, p Avoiding intimacy	e, h, l Anger
i, q, r, v Affection	h, r, v Degradation and hu-
m, q Boredom	miliation
e, i, r, v Depression	h, l Guilt
e, i, l, r Jealousy	h, v Insecurity
e Rebellion	m, q Loneliness
e, i, r, v Poor self-esteem	h, l, r Revenge

3. "Yes" answers to any of the following suggests that one or more of the accompanying nonsexual motives could be entering your sex life.

f, j, k, n, u, x Avoiding inti-	a, b, c, p Anger
macy	w, x Atonement
k, s Affection	a, t, z Barter
s Boredom	p, t, u, z Degradation and hu-
f, k, o, w Depression	miliation
f, s Haven	p, w Guilt
c, k Jealousy	a, f, g, j, k, n, o, s, z Insecurity
a, b, c, k, z Rebellion	k, s Loneliness
b, g, o Poor self-esteem	a, b, j, k, p Revenge
o, u Social pressure	n, u Sexual identity

If you have unsatisfied emotional needs, they are probably affecting your sex life. The following questions will help you determine to what extent they affect your satisfaction.

Respond to the following statements with either Yes or No. Again, be spontaneous and avoid debating your answers.

—— (1) I feel my sex life is exciting.
—— (2) I frequently feel something is wrong with sex.
—— (3) I feel sex should be better.
—— (4) I have sex as often as I would like.
—— (5) I feel I am undersexed.

—— (6) I often have sex just to please my partner.

—— (7) I sometimes fake orgasm.

—— (8) I have trouble achieving orgasm.

—— (9) I have to hold back to keep from climaxing too soon.

—— (10) I wait for my partner to climax first.

—— (11) I like my body.

—— (12) I think I am sexy.

—— (13) I think I am attractive to the opposite sex.

—— (14) I find it easy to talk to members of the opposite sex.

—— (15) I am comfortable when naked.

—— (16) I limit sex to nighttime.

—— (17) I limit sex to the bedroom.

—— (18) I regularly have sex in the same position.

—— (19) My partner can predict my next move.

—— (20) My partner would label me a timid lover.

—— (21) My partner would label me an excessively passionate lover.

—— (22) I frequently fantasize during sex.

—— (23) I sometimes laugh during sex.

—— (24) I sometimes have sex when I am not in the mood.

—— (25) I sometimes have sex when I know I really don't want it.

—— (26) I talk to my partner after sex.

—— (27) I sometimes have sex after an argument.

—— (28) I often have sex when there is nothing else to do.

1. "Yes" answers to questions 1, 4, 11, 12, 13, 14, 15, 23, and 26 suggest that your sex life is relatively free of nonsexual motives.

2. "Yes" answers to any other questions or "No" answers to the ones just listed indicate that interfering nonsexual motives are decreasing your sexual pleasure, satisfaction, or both. The more of your responses that fit in this pattern, the greater the decline.

You now have an idea which nonsexual motives might be influencing your sexual behavior and to what extent they are interfering with your enjoyment. The next step is to discover how and where these unsatisfied needs enter your sex life.

Begin by scrutinizing your own behavior in bed. Divide your sexual behavior into the following categories: (1) what arouses you, (2) foreplay, (3) fantasy, (4) afterplay. Examine each area and look for rigid habits, recurring patterns, or repeating rituals, all of which are symptoms of unsatisfied nonsexual needs surfacing in the bedroom. The following guidelines will help you complete your analysis.

WHAT AROUSES YOU?

Healthy individuals can be aroused by a variety of stimuli. Excessively narrow limits in this area generally indicate a problem. Examples of such limits are listed below, along with the corresponding nonsexual needs that are probably not being satisfied.

- The male who is turned on only by large breasts: look for dependency needs, the need for reassurance, or a low sense of self-worth.
- The person who is turned on only by generous buttocks: watch for avoidance of emotional contact or a disregard for personal interactions.
- A strong preference for mean or unkempt partners: this might indicate a poor self-image, a desire to be humiliated, or repressed aggression.
- A choice of weak or ineffective partners: this reveals a desire to dominate, a need for control and power, or a low sense of self-confidence or self-esteem.
- A choice of excessively large partners: this indicates strong dependency needs, a desire for reassurance and nurturance, or a desire to be dominated.

- An attraction only to masculine women or feminine men: this might mean an unresolved sexual identity or a problem with dependency or passivity.

Basically, your choice of partners and love objects is a reflection of your personality. Very narrow limits imply a constricted personality, but individuals who become aroused over anything and everything may also have serious problems. Healthy individuals can be turned on by a wide variety of stimuli. The key difference between healthy and unhealthy is a freedom of choice. Healthy individuals are not victims of impulse and bodily reaction. They are aware of what is happening and feel they have a choice: they respond according to their preferences and their partner's.

FOREPLAY

Again, healthy individuals enjoy a wide variety of foreplay activities. Excessive restrictions, compulsions, or rituals reflect problem areas, some examples of which are listed below.

- Sex is largely a barrage of kisses from start to finish: look for unsatisfied affectional or reassurance needs.
- No foreplay: look for hostility, resentment, or avoidance of emotional involvement.
- Excessive cursing or vulgarity: this shows the desire to humiliate or hurt.
- Rough handling: this can indicate anger, aggression, the desire to hurt, or a fear of dependency.

FANTASY

Some psychologists and psychiatrists feel that engaging in some fantasy is a sign of a healthy imagination. Others claim that all fantasy detracts from the immediacy and intimacy of sex. Generally, however, fantasy signals an actual problem only when it becomes compulsive or a necessary precursor to sex. It is also detrimental when a single, recurring theme is the focus of the fantasy.

The following are some sample fantasies and the possible motives they mask. Again, problems are indicated only when the fantasy occurs repetitively and compulsively.

- Being watched by others: look for a strong, unsatisfied need for recognition and affection or for confirmation of sexual identity.
- Watching a partner have sex with others: this suggests latent homosexual needs, a desire to humiliate or be humiliated, or a need to be liked.
- Having multiple partners: this might indicate a need for reassurance, a poor sexual or self-identity, the need to be liked and nurtured; it can also camouflage anger toward the opposite sex.
- Having sex with strangers: this suggests an avoidance of emotional contact or a desire to escape from boredom or loneliness.
- Having anal intercourse: look for an avoidance of emotional contact or a desire to hurt or humiliate.

AFTERPLAY

What a person does and thinks about immediately after sex is the most critical indicator of sexual adjustment. The emotions that emerge following the sex act give clues to which, if any, nonsexual motives and needs were operating. As you read the following examples, keep in mind that everyone indulges in almost all of them at one time or another. Look for a habit, ritual, or compulsion.

- Rolling over immediately to sleep: be wary of avoiding

emotional contact, feeling angry, or wanting to escape from your lover.

- Arguing: this suggests smoldering anger, resentment, feelings of being used or abused, or a power struggle.
- Separating to read: you may be trying to escape from boredom, avoid emotional contact, express dissatisfaction, or emphasize a poor interpersonal relationship.
- Rolling over and reading a sexually oriented magazine: this suggests dissatisfaction with your partner or a desire to humiliate and hurt.
- Dashing to the bathroom to wash: this indicates feelings of guilt, that sex is dirty, feeling abused, or avoiding contact and intimacy.
- Wanting or demanding an immediate replay: this suggests an insecure sexual identity, a need for reassurance, a lack of satisfaction, or a desire to dominate and hurt.
- Thinking about chores or the office: this can mean that sex is being used as a reprieve from stress or boredom, or it can be a sign of guilt or low self-esteem.
- Thinking about conquering the world: this may indicate that sex is a prop for a poor self-image.
- Feeling depressed or thinking sad thoughts: this is generally an indication that one or more nonsexual motives are at work.

The healthiest thoughts are those about the experience, your partner, your own pleasure, your relationship, the closeness, the afterglow, or just plain happy thoughts.

In general, any pattern of avoiding contact (sleeping, leaving the room, reading, mentally drifting to other areas) indicates distance or a reluctance to communicate what was really experienced. When a couple has a healthy relationship, afterplay is couple-centered, with continued physical and emotional contact. Some couples fall asleep on top of one another still united: others remain cuddled and share their hopes, dreams, and fantasies. It is a healthy sign when a couple shares and discusses their internal experiences, from a gasped "Wow! That was fantastic!" to a more detailed exploration of each other's unique experience and sensations.

WHEN SEX IS NOT A "WOW"!

Even when sex is not so great, discussing the experience is still important. However, it is easy to become embroiled in defensive exchanges that can make matters worse. Here are some suggestions to help avoid the bickering and maximize the chances for peaceful resolution.

- Never accuse your partner of not satisfying you.
- The partner who feels let down should simply state what he or she experienced.
- Both partners should explore and look for solutions.
- Never assume that something is wrong with you or that it is your fault that your partner was not fully satisfied.
- If either partner is not sexually confident, it is usually better to postpone sensitive discussions. This will preserve the pleasantness of the experience for the partner who did enjoy it.

In closing, it is important to remember that there are no blanket rules, symbols, or special meanings that fit everyone. The meaning a particular object or behavior has in your case is determined by one person—YOU. The examples given in the preceding pages are those most generally encountered, but they do not fit everyone. You are the final judge. No one else, not even a therapist, can assign or give meaning to your experience.

The examples discussed in this book are intended to generate ideas and suggest areas for you to question and examine. Your goal is to separate your emotional needs from your sexual ones, and so prevent the misuse of sex in three important ways: First, sex will not be used as a panacea for neutotic needs. Second, sex will not become the dumping ground for unfinished business. Third, sex will not be used to make up for what is lacking in the rest of your life. Exit neurotic baggage, enter sexual ecstasy—enjoy!

24

Understanding
Sexuality

To understand human sexuality we must define and discriminate between some important concepts, the first of which are pleasure and satisfaction. Pleasure is what is felt and experienced *during* an activity. Satisfaction refers to feelings following the act. Usually, an act well done that satisfies a pre-existing need merits a high degree of satisfaction. An act that is poorly performed and does not satisfy a pre-existing need results in feelings of little or no satisfaction.

Pleasure and satisfaction are two different entities and can be experienced independently of one another. Some activities produce a high degree of satisfaction yet afford very little pleasure. For example, running or swimming can be boring, painful drudgery; so can completing a business report. There may be little pleasure involved in these activities, yet satisfaction can be very high. Alternately, some acts, such as eating a fattening dessert or watching a comedy, can afford a high degree of *pleasure* but yield very little satisfaction.

So it is with sex. Although sexual pleasure and sexual satisfaction are two entirely separate entities, they are often lumped together. This mistake creates confusion and prevents us from examining our sex life in the detail it warrants. Any self-examination of sexual behavior must focus on both of these aspects, beginning with a clear understanding of what each entails.

Sexual pleasure refers to bodily sensations while having sex. Touching, kissing, caressing, and pumping all produce feelings that can be classified as sexually pleasurable.

Sexual satisfaction is what is felt following sex. It occurs on two levels: physical and emotional. Physically, sexual satisfaction results from a release or discharge of the sexual/physical energy and tension that builds during foreplay and reaches its peak just before climax. Orgasm is the sudden, explosive discharge of this accumulated tension and energy. When adequate buildup is followed by complete release, a high degree of physical sexual satisfaction is achieved.

There is also an emotional reaction following sex. You can feel good or bad, frustrated or pleased. If no nonsexual motives were operating, you would have positive feelings after sex is over. You may feel joyful, fulfilled, relaxed, intimate, peaceful; any number of pleasant emotions may surface. If nonsexual motives drove the sex, "post-sex emotions" will usually be negative. You will feel frustrated or unfulfilled. In addition, you may be aware of feeling angry, worthless, humiliated, embarrassed, or abused. Any number of negative feelings may surface, depending on which nonsexual motives were active. Here are some examples:

- Motivated by anger, your partner was excessively aggressive. You end up feeling unfulfilled, abused, and angry or hurt.
- You have sex when you really want affection. You end up feeling frustrated, taken for granted, and that something was missing.

In both cases you did or received something different from what you wanted or needed.

Be aware of how you feel both during and after the act. When you enjoy sex from foreplay through afterplay, your physical and emotional parts are well integrated; your emotional self allows your physical self to fully experience what is happening. All of you is working together toward the same goal: sexual pleasure and satisfaction. There is an adequate buildup of sexual tension, discharge is complete, and satisfaction and fulfillment result.

When nonsexual motives direct the behavior, the physical and emotional parts are out of synchronization. Body and mind are pulling in two different directions—sexual and nonsexual—creating conflict instead of building and discharging tension. For example, when an individual uses sex to alleviate loneliness, the touching and caressing, which are normally directed toward building sexual tension, are rechannelled to mollify loneliness. The body feels and wants sex, but emotionally the person needs to deal with the loneliness. Neither need will be satisfied completely. In this case the nonsexual needs interfered at the buildup stage.

Consider a case where sex was used to alleviate anger. John had several sexual experiences which he described as excellent up to the point of climax: "I pump like crazy, but the climax is always a dud, a letdown, ... I get little pleasure or satisfaction ... lately I end up feeling as if I didn't have sex at all. ... " His wife Jan reported that sex was wonderful for her and that John was a very passionate lover. She loved the vigorous and enthusiastic pumping, the hard squeezing and biting. Lately, though, even she thought it might be a little much, but was hesitant to broach the subject with John.

Indeed, it turned out that the aggressive behavior his wife loved was really an expression of anger. It stemmed from what John called "Jan's inability to handle money." This anger interfered with the discharge of the tension. John had a more than adequate buildup but did not experience a complete release; he could not seem to let go. But what is it that John could not let go?

HOLDING BACK

There are two major causes of incomplete building or releasing of sexual tension and energy. Sex therapists have named them *blocking* and *holding back*. These terms are ill defined, yet they are critical to understanding sexual maladjustment. In this book, holding back refers to feelings—but not sexual feelings. The individual is holding back the release of nonsexual impulses during sex.

Consider John's case above. He was using sex to ventilate angry impulses. The holding back at the point of climax resulted from repressing the angry impulses that came dangerously close to release during pumping. *John was holding back anger, not sex!* He was resisting the impulse to pummel his wife. Had John not held back, he might have attacked her much the same as Hector attacked his wife (see p. 155).

In other words, as John pumped, his body was building tension, not from an intense sexual need but from repressed anger and rage. To attack his wife was totally unacceptable to him, so he had to keep himself from releasing the angry tension. Thus it is understandable that John did not feel relief after he climaxed. The tension from repressed anger was not released to any significant degree. It was still there, and it kept resurfacing whenever he had sex. Once this nonsexual problem was resolved, sexual satisfaction returned. John no longer had to hold back the anger because it was no longer there.

BLOCKING

Now consider blocking. What is an individual like John blocking that is causing sexual dissatisfaction? Sexual feelings? *No!* He is blocking the nonsexual feelings or needs that are attempting to surface and seek satisfaction during sex. The blocker is trying to prevent the nonsexual from seeping into awareness. Blocking and holding back are both defenses aimed at keeping the nonsexual needs, impulses, or feelings out of the sex act. *Blocking* is when the defense prevents the nonsexual from entering awareness, and *holding back* is when it prevents the acting out of the nonsexual impulse or feeling.

John was blocking during foreplay, trying to keep angry thoughts and feelings from surfacing and inhibiting sexual desire. This was relatively easy as his attention was focused on his partner's body and the build up of excitement, but as passion and intensity increased, his conscious control diminished. His body began to take over. As he pumped furiously, angry impulses came dangerously close to exploding. John's body was ready to lash out in anger. Because this would have been totally unacceptable, he had to hold back—not sexual feelings but angry impulses. The net effect: John could not enjoy his climax; he did not feel sexually satisfied; and his angry nonsexual feelings were not resolved or released. But John was aware only of his sexual feelings, so he attributed his dissatisfaction to sexual inadequacy.

In this, as in all cases, the stronger the nonsexual need, the more it interferes with sex. If no nonsexual motives are operating, there is no interference, and pleasure and satisfaction are at their peak.

In sum, sexual satisfaction is both a physical and an emotional phenomenon. Satisfaction is directly related to the degree of harmony between our emotional and physical states at the time we have sex. The more our nonsexual motives or feelings intrude on our sex lives, the less satisfaction and pleasure we experience.

25

Putting Sex in Its Proper Perspective

Almost everyone has had a fantastic sexual experience. Your body felt great; the emotional atmosphere was beautiful. You ended up feeling satisfied and at peace with yourself and your partner. Sex can be intensely exciting, ecstatically pleasurable, and downright wonderful. Too often, however, sex does not reach this level. We seldom attain the kind of joy we know is possible.

Learning to reach sexual fulfillment is not a simple task. It requires self-awareness and close scrutiny of your attitudes and beliefs about sex. Two beliefs that severely hinder sexual enjoyment are: (1) equating love with sex, and (2) separating the "bedroom personality" from the rest of our character. Both concepts can short-circuit sexual pleasure. It is important to clarify them beginning with the love–sex issue.

196

"OF COURSE I LOVE YOU. I JUST HAD SEX WITH YOU DIDN'T I?"

SEX AND LOVE

In our culture love and sex are closely associated. We tend to assume they are synonomous or that one is part of the other. In fact, they are two completely separate and independent entities. Table II demonstrates that the two concepts are indeed separate in origin, function, and goal.

It is important to maintain the distinction between love and sex. If we shackle our sex with love needs, sex will undoubtedly suffer. Why?

- Sex cannot satisfy love needs, nor can love satisfy sex needs, as Table II so aptly demonstrates. Using one to satisfy the other sets up expectations that cannot be fulfilled.

TABLE II

COMPARISON OF LOVE AND SEX

Sex	Love
is hormonally based	has no biological anchor
is concrete, physical, requires physical contact	is abstract, emotional, does not require physical contact
is indiscriminate—desire can be felt for many	is selective—channeled toward one or a few
sexual attraction may be felt toward a complete stranger	you must know someone before you can love him/her
can occur without love	can occur without having sex
has relief of sexual tension as its goal	has growth and closeness as its goals
is satisfied via intercourse	is satisfied via affection and emotional closeness
can be forced on someone	cannot be forced on anyone
can continue only as long as the physical apparatus works	can continue long after the physical apparatus fails
tends to be short-lived in duration	tends to be of long duration
begins in adolescence and continues to physical deterioration	is unrelated to age and physical condition
is satisfied within one's body	is satisfied by going beyond oneself

- We expect the person we love to satisfy many needs besides our sexual ones. If we confuse love and sex it is easier for these other needs to work their way into the bedroom.

- Love is nonsexual (regardless of cultural or religious beliefs). Placing nonsexual demands, for example, affection, on sex inhibits sexual pleasure. This does not mean that love per se spoils sexual pleasure. Love, in fact, often enhances sex. It is only when we demand that sex satisfy love needs that problems develop.

The philosophy on sexual sex and love intended in this book can best be summarized as follows. Sexual sex within a loving relationship is living poetry, a work of art evolving from the ebb and flow of sexual impulses and energies as they intertwine and seek mutual and self satisfaction. Sexual sex creates an even greater bond and sense of intimacy in the love relationship. We reach new levels of awareness of interdependence, and open the door for further sexual growth. We feel satisfied by our discoveries yet feel the beginnings of a hunger and passion for more intimacy, exploration, and bonding; for a union that transcends the mechanics of sex—one that allows us to feel the full power and depth of a sexual union bonded by love and caring. We also experience a quiet, intense calm, knowing that our sexual cores have touched and will touch time and again.

When sexual sex occurs in a caring and intimate relationship, all this can happen. This does not mean that sex and love are synonymous, or that they are mutually exclusive, or that love is necessary to achieve sexual sex. Sexual sex can occur at any time within any relationship—long-term or fleeting. But sexual sex reaches its peak when partners know and care about each other intimately. Care and intimacy add to the intensity of sexual sex, making it a different kind of experience from sexual sex with a "stranger."

You might reasonably ask, "Why does sex seem shallow and meaningless without love?" There are several reasons.

First, many of us have been taught that sex is dirty, animalistic, and undignified. Love is the crutch we use to impart dignity and remove the "dirt" from sex. We forget that we are the ones who put the "indignity" there in the first place.

Second, we consequently learn to feel guilty about having sex without love. Nothing destroys pleasure and satisfaction more completely than guilt. (See pages 65–73.)

Third, the person who loves us satisfies many important nonsexual needs—affection, reassurance, security, and so on. By meeting these needs, this person acquires special importance for us. Having sex with this person *seems* to have more meaning and depth.

Fourth, when growing up we were conditioned to expect love and sex to go together. Naturally, if we expect something that is not forthcoming, we feel disappointed or unfulfilled. If we do not experience love and sex together, we feel disappointed, and sex seems meaningless. IS IT ANY WONDER THAT SEX WITHOUT LOVE SEEMS MEANINGLESS OR WRONG?

Ask yourself this question: What meaning and depth is sex supposed to have? Sex is simply a physical act designed to give pleasure and procreate the species. Its depth is determined by how thoroughly one wishes to explore it, ranging from a wham-bam one-minute race to an extensive mutual exploration. (See the chapter on sexual sex.)

The sex act can have any meaning we wish to place on it, but we tend to forget that we are the ones who impose the meaning. To say that sex is an act of love does not reflect objective reality. It creates confusion. It creates victims.

The most common of these victims is the couple who expect sex to save their weak relationship or marriage. They attempt to use sex to cement the bonds of love. This never works. Sex becomes strained and develops into a new source of conflict, often dealing the death blow to a marriage that might other- wise have been salvaged.

Other victims include the couple who lose sexual attraction for each other, as when one partner gains weight and becomes unappealing. Instead of dealing with two separate issues, love and sexual attractiveness, the couple assumes that, because sex has stopped, love has ended. They give up on the relationship before they examine all the alternatives. Often they continue on together with nothing resolved, living unhappy, unsatisfying lives. The heavy partner feels unloved because no sexual advances are forthcoming; the other partner feels that the added weight indicates a lack of care and concern ("If you loved me you'd lose weight. You'd care enough to make yourself appealing."). The real issues are lost.

We must learn to see that love and sex are not synonymous. Equally important, we must learn to accept all variations and degrees of both. Some couples who have sex, love each other dearly, others not at all. Some couples who are deeply in love have sex very often, others occasionally, and some never. Certainly love can exist without sex just as easily as sex can exist without love. We can enjoy one without the other just as easily as we can enjoy both together.

Separating love and sex does not mean that we should *not* have sex with the one we love, or that we *should* have sex with someone we do not love. It means that the two are separate and distinct needs, and that one can interfere with the fulfillment and satisfaction of the other. But this can happen only when we do not realize that they are independent of one another.

In effect, we must separate our sex needs from our love needs, and resolve each independently. But not necessarily with different people. There is nothing to prevent us from seeking and obtaining sexual satisfaction with the person we love. We simply must be aware of what we are doing and stop blaming one area for the lack of satisfaction in the other. Likewise, we must stop trying to use one to satisfy needs stemming from the other.

THE BEDROOM PERSONALITY

Many of us assume that we have two separate personalities—one we confine to the bedroom; the other we show to the rest of the world. We assume that when we enter the bedroom, we take on a new personality, unshackled by the needs, doubts, and fears of the nonbedroom world. By believing in two separate personalities, we preclude seeing any connection between nonsexual needs and our bedroom behavior. In effect, if we do not believe that there is any connection between the two, we certainly are not going to look for any.

An example will demonstrate the error of such thinking. Consider the common case of a business executive who becomes impotent for a few days prior to a board meeting. Obviously his bedroom personality is not as independent as he would like it to be. Most cases of temporary impotence are proof of the powerful connection between what goes on outside the bedroom and what we do in it. It is foolish to think that we automatically leave our troubles and concerns outside the bedroom door. It can be done but it takes practice and self-discipline.

It is equally foolish to think that major needs—such as affection, security, reassurance, feeling important and in control—cease to exist the minute we hop into bed. In fact, they do not. We usually take them with us right under the covers. We are just not aware of their presence. As long as we are unaware of these needs, they are free to do their damage and rob us of pleasure and satisfaction. The case histories throughout the chapters on nonsexual motives demonstrate how this happens.

The myth of the bedroom personality is so pervasive and so harmful that we should consider why people believe it. Cases like the following seem to lead people to believe in its existence.

Carl came for therapy because he was disillusioned. He had recently married a shy, respectable young woman. Carl said, "I just knew she was a virgin before we married." After the honeymoon he was not so sure. According to Carl, Yvonne turned into a tiger who obviously knew her way around the bedroom. He said, "I swear she was a different person once the lights went out! She's certainly not the one I married—or thought I did. I'm totally confused."

In therapy this couple learned about nonsexual needs and how they can create "the bedroom personality." They learned that Yvonne's shyness elicited affectionate, protective behavior from Carl. Yvonne's needs for affection and security were amply satisfied outside the bedroom. Once under the covers she was ready for action with only minor preliminaries. Carl perceived her anxiousness to get it on as prior experience. In the bedroom, he needed more time to build his confidence and was shocked at Yvonne's readiness in her role as a lover.

Tim and Marion experienced a similar shock. Marion was convinced that Tim had a split personality. Before marriage he had been a kind, considerate individual. In fact, it was his gentleness that attracted Marion and made her decide he was the ideal man. After the ceremony, however, she was introduced to his other half, "a wild, inconsiderate sex maniac."

In therapy they learned Tim's real problem: he did not feel manly. He was kind and considerate to Marion because it made him feel like a man. His bedroom behavior, though quite different, was also designed to prove his masculinity. He assumed that real men were masters of the bedroom and behaved accordingly. Cases like this show how the myth that our bedroom behavior is independent of our "other" personality can be perpetuated.

A second factor contributing to this myth occurs when we confuse the "roles we play" with our personality. We all play many roles in life—worker, parent, citizen, and so on. We do not assume a separate, independent personality for each role. Rather, we act out each role within the confines of our personality. It is when we compartmentalize the roles and fail to integrate them into a unified whole that it seems as if we have many personalities.

A third factor that helps perpetuate the myth of the bedroom personality is that we each like to see ourselves as a superstar in the bedroom, a lover without flaws. To preserve this image we choose not to see our faults. We ignore any suggestion that needs, weaknesses, or worries from outside the bedroom can affect our performance as a lover.

Obviously, increasing self-awareness for the sake of sexual satisfaction must not be limited to a cross-examination of your sex life. You must include an examination of your personality, especially how you express and satisfy your emotional needs. Your goal should be to become aware of these emotional needs, separate them from your sexual needs, and seek their satisfaction independent of sex.

This split between the sexual and nonsexual does not mean that you should develop separate personalities. It means that you should develop awareness of both areas, and deal with the nonsexual outside the bedroom to clear the body and mind of excess burdens. Then you can concentrate on the sexual in the bedroom. For example, if you are anxious about an upcoming board meeting, prepare for it before you have sex. If you are lonely, satisfy your need for companionship before you hop into bed. If you need affection, do not wait until just before the clothes come off—get it as the need arises. In this way these needs are kept at a minimum during the bedroom hours. Sex will not become the supposed cure-all for our neurotic needs or the dumping ground for our unfinished business.

In sum, we must take two steps toward sexual fulfillment. First, we must realize that our personality dynamics operate inside the bedroom just as they do outside. Second, we must free sex of all the irrelevant nonsexual motives and needs that should be satisfied elsewhere, throwing out the emotional baggage that hinders sexual pleasure. This does not mean engaging in wild or mechanical, emotionless sex. It means guarding against using sex to make up for what is lacking in other areas of our lives.

"HARRY HAS A SEX PROBLEM DOCTOR.
HE'S NOT AGGRESSIVE ENOUGH IN BED."

26

Putting It All Together

In closing, two points should be emphasized:

First, if a nonsexual motive enters the bedroom, it does not mean that your sex life is in jeopardy. All human behavior can and does have more than one motive. Consider the following analogy.

John enjoys racquetball. It helps him to stay trim. It may also provide companionship or serve as a release for aggression. As he becomes proficient, the game may also satisfy his need to feel competent, or his need for recognition. All of these motives and needs may influence his game and the sport will still remain pleasurable. However, John's pleasure is maximized when he plays simply because he wants to, because he enjoys it. The more predominant the other motives become, the less enjoyment John derives from playing.

Take a day when John's need to feel competent is at a peak and is driving his game. He misses a few shots and becomes upset. His determination increases but he repeatedly makes mistakes. When the game is over, John feels frustrated, unsatisfied, and has not enjoyed playing as much as usual. If this pattern continues John would eventually give up the game.

So it is with sex. Sex *can* be a vehicle for the expression of

love. It *can* afford companionship and affection. It *can* enhance sexual identity and set the stage for emotional intimacy. However, these are byproducts of the sex act. As long as sex is used primarily to satisfy sexual needs, the act will be pleasurable. We will feel sexually satisfied. As the nonsexual needs become more predominant and drive sexual behavior, satisfaction diminishes. After sex we will feel just as John felt after he played racquetball to feel competent: frustrated and unsatisfied. If we continue to have sex primarily for nonsexual reasons, we will eventually lose interest in sex, just as surely as John would eventually give up racquetball. In effect, when we set out to have sex only to satisfy our need for intimacy, to avoid loneliness, or to seek affection and companionship, to name a few, we misuse sex. We lose pleasure and satisfaction. We slowly undermine our ability to enjoy sex.

Second, do not assume that all individuals or couples have nonsexual themes constantly controlling their sex lives. Sexual relationships that are in trouble and afford little pleasure undoubtedly do, as some of the case histories in the previous chapters show. But most of us do have different nonsexual needs that surface in our bedrooms at one time or another. Thus it is important to be aware of which nonsexual needs we fail to satisfy outside the bedroom so we can minimize their influence on sex and maximize our pleasure and satisfaction. The best way to have a highly satisfying sex life is to make sure our lives *outside* the bedroom are enjoyable and satisfying.

The sex act can only add to, not replace, whatever exists prior to sex. If you feel good about yourself and close to your partner before sex, you will feel better and closer after making love. If you have a negative self-image or feel isolated from or angry with your partner before sex, you will feel worse afterwards. Sex can never bridge the gap of loneliness or be a substitute for other emotional needs. Sex can satisfy sexual needs and nothing more.

So where does all of this leave you? You have learned about a new way to examine your sex life, a new way to find sexual satisfaction that does not emphasize the mechanics of sex. You do not need to learn to stand on your head, become double jointed, or be a sexual athlete. You need only examine your life in and out of the bedroom, and face what lies a little below the surface. You have nothing—absolutely nothing—to lose and everything to gain.

You and your partner will be the sole judge of what is happening in your bedroom. Likewise, both of you will receive the prize that awaits those willing to scrutinize their sexual behavior. The prize? Sexual sex—sex that is more pleasurable and satisfying than you ever thought possible.

* * *

This is a new way to look at human sexuality and examine your own sex life and behavior. If you have any comments or want to share any of your experiences, please contact either of us at: 890 Downingtown Road, West Chester, Pennsylvania 19380.

"NOW LET'S SEE IF I HAVE THIS STRAIGHT. HARRY HERE HAS THIS PROBLEM WHICH IS <u>YOU</u> DON'T ENJOY SEX."

Appendix I

Nonsexual Sex Therapy: General Guidelines

Modern sex therapy typically treats the mechanical side of sex. Through sensate focus, deconditioning, or reconditioning, a couple is taught to increase sexual enjoyment by improving sexual technique. This has been considered a major breakthrough in treatment, with a cure rate said to be as high as 95%. However, we must ask, "What is cured?"

For example, a couple has a problem: neither enjoys sex. If they receive coaching and training from a sex therapist, their technique will improve and they will enjoy sex more. But is the real problem cured? Probably not. Consider the following analogy.

Johnny, age 10, feels inadequate. He has few friends and the children in his neighborhood do not play with him. When a neighborhood baseball team is formed, Johnny wants to play but thinks he is not good enough. He tells his dad he is not going out for the team because he does not really like the sport.

Dad, sensing that Johnny would like the game if he were a better player, coaches and trains him. Johnny becomes better, admits he enjoys the game, and signs up for the tryouts. Is Johnny cured? If you saw his problem as being a poor baseball player who did not like the game, then he was cured. If you saw his problem as a basic lack of self-confidence, then the problem still exists.

So it is with sex therapy. If you see the problem as inadequate or ineffective technique, a therapy that focuses on improving skill will undoubtedly render a cure rate of 95%. The underlying assumption of technique therapy is that couples have sex to experience pleasure. This certainly seems reasonable. Teaching them sex techniques that will add to their pleasure would be a logical way to solve the problem.

However, most dissatisfaction with sex cannot be attributed to a deficiency in skill alone. A change in attitude is almost always more effective than a simple change in procedure. Consider this hyperbolic case.

Roger cannot satisfy his hunger. He complains that he never feels "full" and does not enjoy eating. Let us apply the "technique" reasoning to Roger's problem. People eat because they are hungry and/or enjoy eating. Roger cannot satisfy his hunger and does not enjoy his food. Therefore Roger must not know how to eat properly. He must be taught to eat! We send him to a hunger therapist.

Roger is instructed to enroll in a gourmet cooking class, in an Emily Post manners class, and in a Primal Eating group (where he learns to tear into his food and eat with his hands or feet, whichever strikes his fancy). Well, Roger does notice an increase in enjoyment. The food does taste better (at least when he doesn't use his feet). But alas! Several months after therapy, Roger begins to lose interest again. His bank account has dwindled as a result of the high price of his gourmet food. He is in danger of losing his job because he spends hours preparing fancy meals instead of working. Even worse, he does not like to clean up the mess after dining. Poor Roger! He is right back where he was before, only poorer.

Roger could have gone to a perceptive clinician who would have recognized the real problem: that Roger was, in fact, depressed, and was using eating to satisfy nonhunger needs. Roger would have learned how he was doing this and in 3 to 6 months would have resolved his problems. Not only would he enjoy food more, he would find more satisfaction in all areas of his life. His better emotional adjustment would allow him to be more productive on the job, and his social life would also improve.

This example, of course, is oversimplified and exaggerated. However, it is intended to show how "curing" sex problems at the technique level typically makes only a dent in the total problem. The point is, we typically assume that sex is always aimed at satisfying sexual needs. This is not true. Inadequate, unsatisfying sex suggests that nonsexual motives are at work.

The essence of nonsexual sex therapy is to discover which needs or motives are interfering with sexual pleasure and satisfaction. Why is this important? Why not simply work directly on improving sex and settle for some improvement? It is important to ferret out these hidden motives and needs for two reasons. First, as previously stated, it is the burden of satisfying these hidden needs that restricts sexual pleasure. Second, these hidden motives reflect deficiencies in other areas of the relationship.

If someone is using sex as a means of establishing emotional contact, you can be sure there is little intimacy outside the bedroom. If someone is using sex to feel privileged and important, this need is not being satisfied in other areas. Intimacy and feeling important should develop out of the uniqueness of the relationship, out of the respect and love each partner gives to the other, not out of a good lay.

Focusing on sexual technique prior to untangling these needs short-circuits the process of emotional and sexual maturity. How? If a couple does not separate the sexual from the nonsexual, they can never learn more effective, mature ways of satisfying their nonsexual needs. If they continue to use sex for nonsexual purposes, they cannot fully explore and enjoy their sexual natures. They are doomed to repeat the unsatisfying behavior; their sexual development is arrested at a neurotic level.

The therapist's role should be to help couples discover the hidden needs they are trying to satisfy through sex. Once the nonsexual needs are discovered, the couple can learn to separate and satisfy them outside the bedroom. When this is accomplished, any work or coaching on sexual technique will be a hundred times more effective. The door to intense sexual pleasure will be free to open.

MULTIPLE CAUSES

Nonsexual sex therapy can become quite complicated. There are no rules or formulas to follow. There are, however, some basic guidelines that any therapist using this approach should keep in mind.

1. The same sexual behavior may be motivated by different needs in different individuals. For example, Alan, Sue, and Paul all had extramarital affairs. Alan's motive was to humiliate his wife, who outranked him professionally. Sue was driven by a need to prove her femininity. Paul was out to get revenge for his wife's lack of zeal in bed. Still other motives are possible. The therapist must locate the nonsexual needs of each individual or couple and determine how these needs are influencing sexual behavior.

2. One motive can be satisfied by a number of different behaviors. For example, the desire to humiliate can be satisfied by demanding unconventional sex, by having a fling with a prostitute, or by criticizing technique and making derogatory comments during sex. Wendy's case illustrates this point.

Wendy came for therapy because she could not be satisfied sexually. She loved to kiss—the longer and more passionately, the better. She also liked to be handled very roughly. She was pleased when her lover called her "my personal whore." Her problem turned out to be an insatiable desire to be wanted and needed. As she put it, "when my man grabs me, I know he really wants me. The more passionate he kisses me, the more I feel special. And being his whore . . . well, I guess then I know he needs me." As Wendy became more in touch with her non-sexual needs, sex became more satisfying. She enjoyed sex even more, and felt fulfilled and less driven.

3. One behavior may be caused by multiple motives in the same person. In these cases, it is important to figure out *all* the motives. The couple usually experiences a series of "cures," followed by relapse. Each time a motive is brought to light, the maladaptive behavior subsides; the couple experiences relief and sex improves. But soon the inappropriate behavior resurfaces, and sexual satisfaction declines until the other motives are uncovered.

This is the pattern that emerged in Bob and Wilma's case. They came for therapy because Bob had had an affair. He claimed it meant nothing to him and could not understand why he had done it. He also said that he was happy and satisfied with his marriage of four years. Both he and Wilma seemed to genuinely love and respect each other.

We were puzzled until the following exchange occurred late in the second session. Wilma was instructed to tell Bob exactly how she felt, how the affair affected her.

> *Wilma.* It hurt . . . completely destroyed my faith in you. . . . I can't trust you ever again.
> *Bob.* Ha! Now you know how I felt when I found out about your college days.

Wilma had had sex with several of her previous boyfriends but had never told Bob because she felt it was her own business. Bob was hurt and angry when he found out. He had been a virgin at marriage, and he expected the same from his wife. He felt deceived and wanted revenge.

Once this issue was aired and resolved, their sex life returned to normal. Therapy was terminated as everyone felt the problem had subsided. Seven months later they returned for therapy because Bob had had another affair.

Again he was at a loss to explain his behavior. He did not feel revenge was the motive, and neither did the therapist. As Bob spoke about the affair he told how exciting it was—how it made him feel like a "stud," and how he had never felt like that before. In the next few sessions he talked about his uneasiness around women. He admitted that he had wanted sex before marriage but had been too timid. At times he thought he might be "funny" on men because he felt more comfortable around them.

Bob worked on his sexual identification, and soon became highly confident. Both he and Wilma agreed that sex was never better. Therapy was about to be terminated when Bob called in a panic, confessing an irresistible urge to seduce his wife's best friend. The therapist decided to see him individually (something rarely done in nonsexual sex therapy). As therapy progressed it became apparent that this near affair would have served two purposes. One, Bob was very jealous of Wilma's sociability. She made friends very easily. Everyone spoke highly of Wilma and called her often. She knew everyone's background, aspirations, and problems. Two, Bob wanted to humiliate himself (and probably Wilma, too). In his own words, "Joyce is nothing to look at. I'd even be ashamed to admit I went to bed with someone so. . . . "

The fact that Bob had called and worked at preventing a problem was an indication of the tremendous progress he had made. Therapy continued, individual sessions alternating with joint ones. Bob had some deep-seated problems that had nothing to do with sex, yet had surfaced and almost destroyed his sex life and marriage.

This case was long and complicated, with therapy continuing over a two-year period. Bringing the nonsexual issues to light had a compounding effect. First, it allowed Bob to mature emotionally. As a result, all aspects of the marital relationship improved and became more satisfying. Second, sex became infinitely more enjoyable for both partners. No amount of technique therapy would have produced the same results.

In less complicated cases, equally effective results can be obtained in a shorter period of time, as Peg's case illustrates. Peg, age 24, came for therapy after a scare over herpes. She had slept with several men in the past six months. She spoke of how lonely city life was, and how impersonal people were. It seemed that she was using sex to fight loneliness. As she learned to cope with being alone, her drive to sleep around subsided.

Then the symptoms reappeared. For Peg, sleeping around also satisfied her need for recognition and her need to confirm her sexual appeal. Once these issues were brought to light and resolved, her relationships became more stable and meaningful. She also enjoyed sex much more. Peg began developing more personal resources to cope with city life and her need for recognition. Once again, it is doubtful that "technique therapy" would have accomplished as much in her case.

4. Nonsexual sex therapy begins with the premise that all problems, no matter how one-sided they may seem, are mutual problems. They are mutual because (a) When one partner is not satisfied or happy, the other partner is also affected. (b) The particular problem would not exist outside the relationship. It exists only because one or both partner's nonsexual needs are not satisfied outside the bedroom. (c) Even though sexual satisfaction is each partner's own responsibility, the commitment implied in any loving, long-term relationship is to help each other.

All problems are mutual, even when one partner initially seems to be the sole culprit. Careful scrutiny of the relationship will bring to light the role each partner plays in perpetuating the problem.

"DOCTOR, HARRY HAS THIS SERIOUS PROBLEM. EVERY TIME ANOTHER MAN LOOKS, TALKS OR SMILES AT ME HE FLIES INTO A RAGE. LIKE IT'S MY FAULT OR SOMETHING."

Ray and Laura are a good example. They came for therapy because of Ray's fits of jealousy. He would become annoyed and sometimes sulk for days when another man paid attention to Laura. Laura told her tale of woe; how badly she felt for Ray; how uncomfortable and embarrassing it was when Ray blew up in public; how she feared he might get hurt by one of her bigger admirers. Meanwhile this coy young lady displayed lip-licking and pursing, leg-crossing, rump-shifting, and chest-thrusting that made the best of Madison Avenue look inept.

Both partners agreed that Ray had a serious problem, but they did not see it as a joint issue. In fact, Ray *did* have a problem. He felt that Laura was a very attractive woman and he was not sure he could hang on to her. He was insecure and felt threatened by the attention other men paid to her. Failing to appreciate the importance of other aspects of a healthy relationship, such as love, support and close emotional contact, he focused only on sex and the lust of other men who might lure Laura away from him. Certainly Ray had a problem.

But so did Laura! She was very insecure and needed constant reassurance of her attractiveness. She encouraged the passes from other men in order to make Ray jealous. As she later said, "The more upset he got, the more I felt reassured. I guess it's childish, but I was secretly pleased. I felt like I was really important to him."

The problem was neither Ray's nor Laura's. Both had a problem: a lack of trust, intimacy, and emotional contact. Of course, not all cases are so obvious. Sometimes pathologies are very subtly intertwined and enmeshed. The point is that no one should ever assume that one partner owns the problem, no matter how obvious it seems. Both are partners in the relationship. Each is affected by the behavior of the other. The key question is: *Which hidden needs are being satisfied by each partner's behavior?*

5. Some nonsexual motives can, and do, seem similar. For example, using sex for barter and to dominate your partner have a similar goal. The individuals are out to get their own way. In the former, one partner takes the other into consideration and control is a side issue. In the latter, control *is* the issue, with one partner striving to get his/her way regardless of the needs of the other.

The case is the same with jealousy and revenge. It can be argued that the vengeful partner is jealous, which is probably partially true. However, in jealousy the issue tends to be a sense of insecurity. The central issue in revenge is the desire to hurt or get even.

Finally, consider using sex as a haven. The couple that does this must be made aware of what it is they are trying to escape. They may be seeking a refuge from boredom, the rat race, stress, tension, reality, closeness—any number of things.

This book has attempted to delineate as many of the more

common motives as possible. Some overlap is inevitable. The role of the therapist is to help untangle the emotional net in which couples trap themselves. If this seems complicated or cumbersome, remember that delineating issues and making fine discriminations is the essence and art of therapy.

The goal of nonsexual sex therapy is to direct the client toward sexual sex without nonsexual baggage. To accomplish this, the therapist must help the couple establish a pattern for satisfying nonsexual needs outside the bedroom. As some of the cases in previous chapters demonstrated, this may bring about sweeping changes in relationships. As we have also seen, what seems to be a sex problem may have little to do with sex. Most couples are relieved to discover that there is nothing wrong with their capacity to enjoy sex.

Appendix II

Nonsexual Sex Therapy: Goals and Considerations

Progress in nonsexual sex therapy is smooth and rapid once the nonsexual motives are uncovered. There is, however, a problem for which every therapist should be prepared: as the couple becomes aware of their nonsexual motives for having sex, there is usually a change in the frequency of sex.

Some nonsexual motives, for example, the need to confirm sex appeal, keep sexual activity at an artificially high level. Individuals driven by this type of motive have sex more often than they really want to. Once this motive is removed from the bedroom, they usually experience an initial decline in sexual frequency; they begin to avoid sex whenever they realize it would be used to satisfy this nonsexual need. This may be quite frightening to some individuals; they may fear they are losing their sex drive. They are afraid that sex will never be the same, that their sex life is ruined. In truth, it is to be hoped that sex *will* never be the same. It will be *better*, not ruined. It is important to discuss this with the client.

In many cases the decline is only temporary. Once the non-sexual issues subside, the true force and power of the unencumbered sex drive will surface. Sex will establish its own cycle, its own ebb and flow, and will be immensely more pleasurable. If anything is lost in quantity, the improved quality will more than make up for it. Nonetheless, the therapist must prepare the client for any anticipated changes in sexual behavior. Inadequate preparation invites resistance to the therapeutic process. The client is likely to end therapy if he/she does not understand the changes.

Some nonsexual motives inhibit sexual activity; for example, withholding sex to get even for hurt feelings. Removing this motive from the bedroom increases the frequency of sex. This usually does not present a problem. Most clients are pleased with such results.

In general, nonsexual sex therapy does not involve an emphasis on technique or frequency. Advice is seldom given; nor is any type of activity encouraged or discouraged. Clients are allowed to determine what is right for them. The therapist's role is to help uncover the nonsexual motives that are detracting from sexual pleasure and satisfaction.

How common are sex problems? Or, more correctly, "How common are hidden motives in sexual behavior?" It is very likely that in most relationships the nonsexual and sexual are intertwined and interfering with sexual enjoyment. Does this mean that most people have terrible sex lives? No! But it does mean that most of us do not achieve the level of sexual pleasure and satisfaction we are capable of experiencing.

Why don't more people seek therapy? First, most of us are not aware of how much pleasure and satisfaction we are missing—you cannot know what ecstasy is unless you have experienced it. Second, in many cases the nonsexual motives of one partner complement and are compatible with those of the other partner. John and Pauline's case is an example.

John used sex as a haven from the rat race, seeking comfort and reassurance from Pauline. She wanted affection and needed to feel important. The more Pauline comforted John, the more affectionate and grateful he became. She, in return, felt important and appreciated. Each satisfied the other's nonsexual needs superbly and both felt their sex life was fine. Neither partner was aware that sex could be better. Their problems began when Pauline had a "one-night stand" that was a real sizzler. Suddenly the possibility of true sexual pleasure was realized.

Couples are most likely to seek help when one partner's hidden motive is at odds with the other partner's. For example, one partner may use sex to confirm sexual identity, the other to satisfy affectional needs. The former will want passionate, intense sex, while the latter will want kisses and caresses.

The actions of one will turn off the other. The partner with the weak sexual identity will feel like a failure because the other does not return the passion and wants to stay at the necking stage; the partner who wants affection will feel used, unloved, and perhaps a little frightened by the other's zeal. Fighting and mutual accusations become more frequent as their sex life deteriorates. Sex will be blamed for a problem that had little to do with sex.

Fred and Martha had this problem. The following excerpt is taken from their third session.

Fred. Sometimes I think I'm in bed with a little girl.
Martha. Oh yeah? Sometimes I *know* I'm in bed with a big oaf!
Therapist. (interrupting a string of nasty exchanges) Let's back up a bit. Fred, you said, "Sometimes I think I'm in bed with a little girl." Can you explain that?
Fred. Sure. All she wants to do is kiss and kiss and kiss. It's like I'm with an adolescent who doesn't want to go all the way, just neck.
Therapist. What would you like?
Fred. I want action. I want to see her turn on like crazy. Like she's hungry for me. . . .

Martha. (interrupting) Yea! That's all you want. You just want to stick it in, pump and come. Like you're some kind of stud and I'm supposed to worship your prick or something.

Therapist. Martha, what would you like?

Martha. Love and affection. That's what I want. That's what's important to me.

Therapist. Do you see what's going on here? Fred, you try to use sex to feel like a man, to prove your virility. Martha, you try to use sex to get affection and reassurance. Both of you end up turned off and withdrawing from sex. What we need to do is separate each of your needs from sex . . . see how they can be satisfied outside the bedroom. Then you won't have all that excess stress ruining your fun. How does that sound?

"LET ME RECAPITULATE. YOU FOLKS HAVEN'T HAD SEX IN 15 YEARS, UNDRESS IN THE CLOSET, SHOWER WITH YOUR BATHING SUITS ON AND YOU'RE UPSET BECAUSE SEX HASN'T GOTTEN BETTER SINCE YOUR FIRST SESSION LAST WEEK."

Fred and Martha were amazed. They felt that they finally understood what was going on in the bedroom. They were also relieved to learn that neither had a sex problem. For the duration of therapy very little was said about the mechanics of sex. Instead, the couple and the therapist examined manliness: what it meant to Fred and how he could experience it. They looked for ways Martha could get her share of affection outside the bedroom. Both partners would need to help each other in these areas so that sex would not become a tug of war over whose nonsexual needs were going to be satisfied.

This case illustrates two important points. First, sex therapy can easily proceed beyond the mechanical, coaching stage. The therapist could have used a technique-oriented therapy and coached Fred and Martha on their foreplay skills. Undoubtedly their sex life would have improved. Fred *might* have felt more masculine because he would have become a more proficient lover. As a result, his wife *might* have responded more intensely. This also would have helped Fred to feel more masculine. Martha *might* have found ways to get affection outside the bedroom, or her husband *might* have started kissing more during sex. In either case, sex *might* have become more enjoyable.

But this is leaving too much to chance. If the couple is not made aware of these nonsexual needs, they will rarely learn to satisfy them outside the bedroom. And as the cases throughout this book show, learning to satisfy the needs outside the bedroom *is* the cure.

The second point is that the therapist's role is primarily to help the couple delineate and explore issues. By focusing on the nonsexual motives, not only did Fred's and Martha's sex life improve, they came to understand themselves and each other better.

Notice that each partner already had a pretty good feel for what was happening. Fred felt that he bedded with a little girl who just wanted to kiss; Martha was conscious of the excessively macho approach Fred preferred. They had all the pieces but simply could not put them together. Each blamed the other for the problem without understanding the meaning or purpose of his/her own behavior. This is what happens in most marriages. Each partner is aware of what is "wrong" with the other, but is blind to his/her own behavior and its meaning (another reason why a therapist is helpful).

Some final comments:

- Why leave these important matters to chance?
- Do not assume that solving a concrete technique problem will make the more important nonsexual needs disappear.
- Any limitation placed on a couple's sex life should be imposed by the couple, not by the therapist.
- Left to their own devices, most couples are ingeniously creative at developing their own technique, *once the hidden motives are exposed and resolved.*
- Therapy need not be long-term. It took Fred and Martha three sessions to come to the realization that their problem was not really a sexual one, that they were simply using sex to satisfy nonsexual needs. By their sixth and final session they reported that sex was "just unbelievable. We never thought it could be so much fun . . . not in our wildest fantasies."

In summary, nonsexual sex therapy de-emphasizes technique, focusing instead on the hidden motives that prevent sexual enjoyment. By separating these needs and satisfying them outside the bedroom, we open the door to true sexual ecstasy. Therapists who focus on technique *do* increase sexual pleasure. *But* they also merely widen the trap in which couples are caught, and run the risk of driving the hidden nonsexual needs further into the background, blocking them out of awareness. Emphasizing technique as the problem and the cure limits the pleasure that sex ultimately can deliver.

Bibliography

Barbach, Lonnie. *For Each Other: Sharing Sexual Intimacy*. Garden City, NY: Doubleday, 1983.

Benoit, Hubert. *The Many Faces of Love: The Psychology of the Emotional and Sexual Life*. New York: Octogon, 1980.

Berman, Steve and Weiss, Vivian. *Relationships*. New York: Hawthorne Books, 1978.

Calderone, Mary S. and Johnson, Eric W. *The Family Book about Sexuality*. New York: Harper and Row, 1981.

Centers, Richard. *Sexual Attraction and Love: An Instrumental Theory*. Springfield, IL: Charles C. Thomas, 1975.

Cook, Mark and McHenry, R. *Sexual Attraction*. New York: Pergamon, 1978.

Dauw, Dean. *Stranger in Your Bed: A Guide to Emotional Intimacy*. Chicago: Nelson-Hall, 1979.

Eysenck, M.J. *The Psychology of Sex*. London: J.M. Dent, 1979.

Geer, James et al. *Human Sexuality*. Englewood Cliffs, NJ: Prentice-Hall, 1984.

Greeley, Andrew. *Sexual Intimacy*. Chicago: Thomas More Press, 1982.

Kaufman, Sherwin A. *Sexual Sabotage: How to Enjoy Sex in Spite of Physiological and Emotional Problems*. New York: Macmillan, 1981.

Leonard, George. *The End of Sex*. Los Angeles: Jeremy P. Tarcher, 1983.

Masters, William H. and Johnson, Virginia E. *The Pleasure Bond: A New Look at Sexuality and Commitment*. Boston: Little, Brown and Co., 1970.

McCarthy, Barry W. and McCarthy, Emily. *Sexual Awareness*. New York: Caroll and Graf, 1984.

Milonas, Rolf. *Fantasex: A Book of Erotic Games for the Adult Couple*. New York: Putnam Publishing Group, 1983.

Offit, Avodah K. *The Sexual Self* (revised ed.). New York: Condon and Weed, 1983.

Pietropinto, Anthony, and Simenauer, Jacqueline. *Husbands and Wives: A Nationwide Survey of Marriage*. New York: Times Books, 1979.

Randell, John. *Sexual Variations*. Lancaster, PA: Technomic, 1976.

Robinson, Paul. *The Modernization of Sex*. New York: Harper and Row, 1976.

Sanchez, Gail and Gerbino, Mary. *Let's Talk about Sex and Loving*. Burlingame, CA: Down There Press, 1983. (For children.)

Schwartz, Bernard et al. *Raising Your Child to Be a Sexually Healthy Adult*. Englewood Cliffs, NJ: Prentice-Hall, 1982.

Singer, June. *Energies of Love: Sexuality Revisited*. Garden City, NY: Doubleday, 1983.

Talese, Gay. *Thy Neighbor's Wife*. New York: Doubleday, 1980.

Index

Adolescents, 21, 52, 137–139,
   150–151
   perpetual, 138–140
Affection, 6, 10–14, 147, 185
Afterplay, 187–189
Anger, 6, 74–80, 85–86, 91,
   112–113, 146–147, 153–154,
   156, 185–188, 193
   general, 74–76
   toward partner, 76–79
Appreciation, self, 14, 64
Arguments, 16–19
Arousal, 185–186
Assertiveness, 57
Atonement, 31–37
Attitudes, 48, 149–151, 165, 210

Barter, 108–110
Bedroom personality, 202–204
Blocking, 194–195
Boredom, 98–104, 146
   affairs and, 103
   fear of, 102

Cage building, 19–21
Children, 51–53, 149–151
Closeness, 167, 171
Communication, 33–34, 85,
   189–190
Conditional sex, 110–114
Conditioning, 145–151, 152
   in vivo, 148
   verbal, 147–148
   visual and fantasy, 146–147

Data, sexual, 7–8, 119–122
Degradation, 147
Dependency, 68–69, 127, 136, 185
Depression, 125–131, 148–149
Dominance and control, 105–114,
   185–188

Ethics, code of sexual, 136–137
Expressiveness, 89

Fantasy, 114, 186–187
Favors
   nonsexual, 110
   sexual, 109
Femininity, 49
Fence mending, 15–16
Fidelity, 38–45
Foreplay, 112, 186
Frequency, 48, 120, 163–165,
   219–220
Frigidity, 78–79

Gadgets, 21
Gender identity, 49
Growth
    emotional, 35, 166–167, 171,
        179–180
    sexual, 168–170
Guilt, 62–63, 65–73, 137
    over having sex, 68–70
    over not having sex, 66–68

Hoarding sex, 43–44
Hobbies, 96, 98–101
Holding back, 156, 194–195
Hypersexuality, 50–53

Identity
    gender, 49–53
    sexual, 46–49, 53, 148,
        185–186
Impotence, 78
Inconsideration, 77
Interest, loss of, 78–79, 162
Intimacy, 15–23, 148, 179–180,
    185
Irresponsible partner, 32

Jealousy, 87–96, 167–168
    intercouple, 94–96
        attention from others, 94
        attention to inanimate
            objects, 95
        careers and hobbies, 96
    intracouple, 87–94
        past partners, 93
        sexual enjoyment, 87

Loneliness, 24–30, 148
    married person and, 27–30
    sex and, 4–5
    single person and, 25–27
Love, 134, 197–201

Marriage, 11, 200

Martini, sexual, 115–118
Masculinity, 49
Masters and Johnson, 7–8
Masturbation, 129
Maturity, sexual, 165–166
Modeling and learned attitudes,
    149–151
Moral inhibition, 68–69
Motivation, 7, 211–215
Mutuality of problems, 215–217

Natural flow, 50
Nonsexual sex (defined), 3–4,
    155–156

Oversatiation, 33–34, 38–41

Parental pressure and influence,
    51–53, 65, 149–150
Peer (social) pressure, 150–151
Perpetual adolescent, 137
Perversion, 121
Pleasing others, 61
Pleasure, loss of sexual, 5–6, 161,
    191
Post-ceremony letdown, 133–134
Promiscuity, 59–60

Questionnaire, 181–184

Rape, 5
Rebellion, 132–141
Reich, Theodore, 70–71
Relaxation, 115–118
Religion, 68
Repetition compulsion, 70–71
Repressed needs, 6–7, 74–76, 137
Responsibilities, 31–34
Revenge, 81–86, 147
    active, 82–84
    passive, 84–85
Risk taking, 168–170

Satisfaction, sexual, 168–169, 191–195
Self-esteem, 55–64, 68–69, 91, 127, 129, 154–155, 185–188
Self-sabotage, 60–61
Sex drive
  discrepant, 91, 110
  low, 91–93, 112
Sex therapy
  nonsexual, 211–224
  technique, 8, 47, 69–70, 209–211
Sexual sex, 175–180, 199
Socialization, 3
Social pressure, 119–124
Standards, personal, 137–141
Stereotypes, 35–36
Swinging, 31

Table I, Nonsexual Needs Which

Can be Linked to Sexual Behavior, 158
Table II, Love and Sex, 198
Target behavior, 105, 108
Television, influence of, 120, 151
Timidity, 90
Twin couples, 106–107

Unfinished business, 74, 152–160, 204
Unsavory partners, 57–58
Unsavory sex, 58–59

Variety, 41–42

Weekend sex, 43
Withholding sex, 77, 94–95, 102–103
Workhorse, bedroom, 32, 111, 114